thrift

Bridget Bodoano

photography by Graham Atkins Hughes

Quadrille

thrift

how to have a stylish home without breaking the bank

First published in 2005 by

Quadrille Publishing Limited

Alhambra House

27–31 Charing Cross Road

London WC2H 0LS

Cataloguing-in-Publication Data: a catalogue record
for this book is available from the British Library.

ISBN 1 844001 42 3

Printed and bound in China

Editorial Director **Jane O'Shea**
Creative Director **Helen Lewis**
Art Director and Designer **Mary Evans**
Project Editor **Lisa Pendreigh**
Photographer **Graham Atkins Hughes**
Picture Researcher **Samantha Rolfe**
Illustrator **Bridget Bodoano**
Production Director **Vincent Smith**
Production Controller **Rebecca Short**

introduction

Suddenly, it's smart to be thrifty. For some time, the 'fashionistas' have been wearing second-hand clothes, and top designers have been seen scouring charity shops for garments not only to wear but also to provide them with ideas. Conspicuous consumerism is no longer quite so cool: keeping up with the trends is exhausting, to say nothing of the effect on your bank balance. Prudent people are looking to moderate their desires, and, in some cases, change their lives.

Reasons to be thrifty vary from a wish to be stylish on a restricted budget, through to the rejection of materialism and recognition of the need to cut down for the sake of the planet. Whether you are strapped for cash on the way up or downshifting to a simpler existence, a thrifty approach can help to save not only money but time, energy and possibly your sanity.

Thrift is more than spending less; it is spending wisely. Now this may sound like something your disapproving elders would preach,

but in a world where retail has become a leisure activity, it is difficult not to be tempted by all the goodies on sale. We've all, at some time, bought a load of cheap stuff that, if we're honest, turned out to be a waste of money. If you added up the cost of all the items that you have bought and did not live up to your expectations, you would find that for the same money you could have bought that thing you really coveted but didn't buy because it was too expensive.

Thrift is not about penny-pinching and deprivation; it is about getting the most for your money, using both wit and wisdom and having fun at the same time.

thrifty style

This chapter gives tips not only on keeping up appearances on a small budget, but investing wisely for long-term benefit. Though interiors are now subject to the vagaries of fashion, you don't have to be a slavish follower – or a big spender – to have a home that shows you are

on the fashion ball. Just as it is possible to put together your own style using a mixture of chain store and designer labels, plus a few choice accessories, applying the same approach to interiors can result in a home that suits you well.

make the most of what you've got

The proliferation of current TV shows and magazines focused on interiors sometimes makes it seem that the only route to a stylish interior is through chucking away everything and carrying out extensive building works, whereas, in reality, something as simple and cheap as a coat of paint can achieve quite startling results.

Familiarity with your home and possessions can make you less appreciative of their good points and, for the sake of change, they are often replaced with something that is inferior. A horrible carpet can taint an entire house and make you feel that you need to move; simply taking it up to reveal chic wooden

floorboards can make both you and your home look and feel better. Before committing to expensive building works or replacements, take a good look at what you have.

thrifty consumer
With the ever-increasing availability of affordable good design, the difficulty lies not in finding something to purchase but knowing what to buy. Some items are not always quite the bargain they appear to be, while others can offer astonishingly good value. This chapter provides a guide to the best buys, from what to purchase, where to shop and how to make your acquisitions work well.

make do and amend
In order to make the most of what you've got, you may have to embark upon a schedule of repairing, reviving, reinvigorating or reinventing not only your existing possessions but your home too. First look at the big picture to assess what needs to be done to bring your whole home up to scratch. Assess your aspirational ideals and consider any projects and procedures that will enable you to transform the less than ideal into something highly desirable.

frugal fabrics
Curtains, blinds, cushions, throws and upholstery fabrics are not just finishing touches, they have a huge impact on an interior, especially in living rooms and bedrooms.

Whether you opt for the natural simplicity of plain cottons and linens, the luxury of thick wools, velvets and silks or employ a more decorative approach using patterns and prints, the thrifty way is to use good-quality, inexpensive materials for the background and invest in beautiful, more extravagant fabrics that play a leading role in the larger scheme of things.

Sewing makes a comeback and, as well as ideas for curtains, cushions and throws, there are instructions for a baggy chair cover – an easy-to-make, not-too-expensive makeover for the good, the bad and the ugly.

save energy
Thrift extends beyond your pocket to your personal wellbeing and the environment. The world needs to be thrifty in its use of resources, which are rapidly depleting in the face of rampant consumerism. Looking at ways of reducing, reusing and recycling have become matters of urgency, as well as expediency. Considering the balance of nature, not just that of your bank account, can also have a beneficial effect on your lifestyle, and taking a new look at how you use your own resources could lead to a different way of life altogether.

thrift – what's it all about?

It is easy to reject the concept of thrift as it conjures up images of worthy frugality and a rigorous regime of making do or going without, but there is much more to it than that. Spending less while still having fun and being stylish is not impossible. A fast-moving, ever-changing world means that economic uncertainty can strike at any time, so even if you have no immediate need to give up your consuming passions there is no harm in practising a little prudence and contemplating the wider implications of adopting a thrifty approach to life.

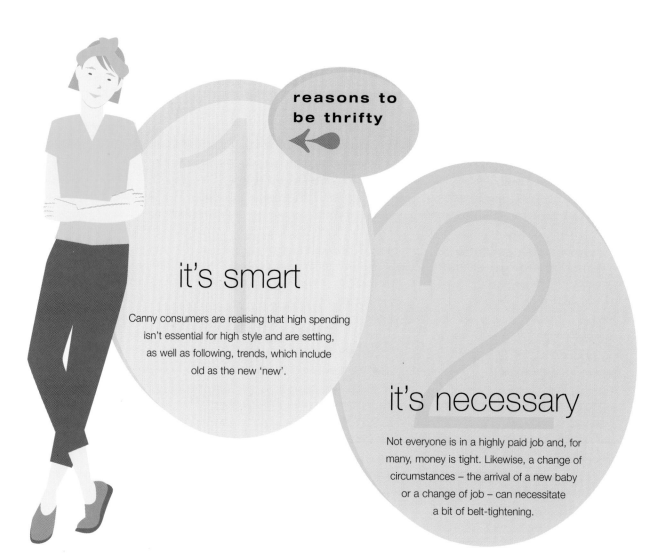

reasons to be thrifty

it's smart

Canny consumers are realising that high spending isn't essential for high style and are setting, as well as following, trends, which include old as the new 'new'.

it's necessary

Not everyone is in a highly paid job and, for many, money is tight. Likewise, a change of circumstances – the arrival of a new baby or a change of job – can necessitate a bit of belt-tightening.

it's good for the world

You don't have to be an anorak to be aware that we can't continue with the vicious cycle of consuming and throwing away that pervades Western society. It may make the economy go round, but it is not so good for the planet. More and more people are wanting to do their bit by recycling, buying eco-friendly and sustainable products and considering alternative sources of power.

it's good for you

The pressures of high consumption can have a deleterious effect on both physical and mental health. Avoiding the pressures of 'keeping up' helps keep down debt, while downshifting is no longer seen as failure, but is acknowledged as a better way of doing things.

it's a question of priorities

Money and time spent on the home means less money and time for other things. Taking a thrifty approach can free up funds for holidays, keeping fit, culture, entertainment and hobbies. It could also allow you to invest in learning and retraining, which could lead to a better job or just a refocusing of priorities.

thrifty style

The material things in life cost money, but style is free. Smart people achieve stylishness through a combination of prudence and panache to turn high street into high fashion and second-hand into swish and swanky. With a few rules plus a dash of imagination, it is possible to create a look that suits you, your home and your bank balance.

smart tricks less is more

While the more extreme examples of minimalism have been eschewed in favour of practicality and comfort, the legacy of architect Mies van der Rohe's philosophy of 'less is more' lives on in a variety of interior styles. Cathartic, decluttering exercises have beneficial effects on individuals as well as their homes; the fashion for paring down has introduced a new, simpler feel to our home furnishings and decoration. And what's more, less costs less.

resist temptation

There are so many well-designed, good-looking, inexpensive products available that it is easy to give in to the temptation to buy more than you really need. A visit to the out-of-town furniture store can soon develop into an orgy of buying; decisions on what to purchase are often clouded by the sheer cheapness of the items on offer, resulting in an unruly assemblage of small, disparate objects rather than a more considered and coherent collection. This can lead to a nasty shock at the checkout with the realisation that, cheap though the individual items may be, buying a lot also costs a lot more. To avoid inadvertent over-spending, have a clear idea of what you need before you go. Make a shopping list and stick to it. If something is out of stock, don't rush into buying the next best alternative. It is better to place an order and wait for the item that you really want rather than plump for what will 'do for now.'

space to breathe

Rather than overcrowding a room, giving furniture some space allows for greater appreciation of its attributes. The new country cottage style is less chintz and cosiness and more natural materials and spare furnishings, favouring sparsely occupied rooms that celebrate the inherent character and raw honesty of stone, wood and metal.

Traditional interiors give precedence to handsome possessions: taking away the distracting competition of less imposing items ensures that the finer pieces stand out against plainer backgrounds. Even those who prefer the exuberance of more exotic interiors are pruning their possessions in order to increase their appreciation of the best of what's left.

patience rewarded

We live in a consumer culture where saving up to buy something seems quaintly old-fashioned. Today's easy and instant access to credit means you no longer have to sit on orange boxes until you can afford chairs; instead, moving into a new home that is fully furnished down to the last vase has become the rule rather than the exception. While it is understandable to want a home that is comfortable and fully equipped, the practice often involves rushing into decisions and making do with cheaper options, leading to a look that is a result of compromise rather than conviction.

Building up a collection of furniture and furnishings over a number of years can be a positive experience, and every new, carefully chosen item will be considered and appreciated that little bit more. Good design is timeless, and investment in a few high-quality classics makes sound thrift sense as they will provide a solid basis on which to build. Take time to decide exactly what you want and if it isn't readily available be prepared to wait for it to turn up in the shop, at a saleroom or on the World Wide Web.

5 stylish shortcuts

Thrift is not only about what's cheap – investing a little more in one item you adore is a better way to spend your money than buying lots of inexpensive things you don't love but feel you ought to have.

For the cost of several budget buys, invest in one beautiful piece that will last and may even appreciate in value.

One or two good-looking items will always look better than a motley assortment of the not-so-nice.

Building a collection slowly over time lessens the likelihood of impulse purchases and mistakes, increasing the quality of your possessions. If in doubt, don't.

When there are fewer objects in a room, more attention is focused on their surroundings. Make sure the backdrop stands up to scrutiny. Plain walls and floors work well, but even if you prefer pattern, keep the space uncluttered, clean and cared for.

Expand your colour search beyond paint charts and swatches. Take ideas and inspiration from a collection of objects.

The colours in this palette include the subtle tones of a glazed pot and delicate shades of a rose. The exuberant cushion complements the wool throws and is tempered by the pale wallpaper. The postcard offers complementary, subdued alternatives.

smart tricks colour scheming

Clever and considered use of colour can make the prosaic look sophisticated, harmonise a chaotic house, draw together a motley collection of furnishings and, if necessary, detract from the imperfect.

colour code

Chain-store clothes shoppers wear a lot of black because the alternative colours on offer often look cheap. It's only when you pay more you get those subtle and unusual colours that look pricey and chic. The same goes for furniture and accessories, but for 'black' read 'neutral'. An inexpensive sofa upholstered in a natural colour can either stand alone or merge into the background, but dress it in harsh bright colours and it will be shown up for what it is.

As with clothes, fashionable colours for interiors can also prove expensive. But, as clever clothes shoppers know, adding a scarf, bag or belt in a new colour can update a classic outfit. Similarly, thrifty decorators can use large expanses of seemingly expensive colour in the affordable form of paint, which can turn an ordinary room into an extraordinarily elegant environment.

classy hues

Look to the posh fashion labels for colour inspiration and, if you dare, take your paint charts into the shops to match up the latest shades. Stores often display clothes grouped in families of colours and tones, as well as patterns and textures, so you should be able to find something to suit your taste. Note how the clothes are accessorised with splashes of other colours, use this information to put together a palette to form the basis of your own interior scheme. You can even take a favourite jumper along to some paint departments where they can reproduce the exact colour.

For a classy look, choose muted neutrals such as taupe, warm greys, pale grey-greens and sage green. Instead of unforgiving pure white, think ivory or bone. Avoid primary colours as cheap versions are rarely good, but if you want bold statements go for fruity hues such as canteloupe, tangerine, strawberry pink, banana yellows and a refreshing squeeze of lime.

Reject sugary pastels in favour of colours with a cashmere aura – soft, pale pinks, blues and greens. If you want dark colour, go for charcoal greys, not black, and think rich, deep purples and reds and matt cobalt blues.

posh accents

If you, or your home, can't cope with too much colour, then introduce small amounts through accessories such as cushions and throws, objects and pictures or a single piece of furniture. These colour accents not only cheer up a neutral scheme but also help to unify an interior, giving an impression of careful co-ordination that could run throughout the whole house as well as just one room. It is possible to integrate an odd chair plus a mirror or picture frame into the scene with a coat of paint in the same colour. However, don't overdo the one colour accent as it can look bitty and contrived, use no more than two distinctive colours and mix with shades or tones of just one of them.

smart tricks accessorising

Smart people can transform last year's clothes into this season's look with a few carefully chosen accessories. Likewise, a few well-chosen extras can lift, enhance or detract from the shortcomings of a dull piece of furniture or the listlessness of a tired room.

shawls and throws

Cosy up with a cashmere throw or change the mood with a silky fringed shawl. Large throws can cover a multitude of sins and disguise a tatty sofa. Knitted throws and blankets tend to hug furniture snugly and look neater, Avoid the 'bedspread' look by using fashionable layers of smaller throws, mixing tones and textures.

cushions and bolsters

A new cushion cover in this season's colours will demonstrate your sharp eye for what's now and save you the trouble and expense of a complete makeover. Impart a bohemian air to a shabby chair or sofa with brightly coloured, embroidered cushions in ethnic fabrics. Regularly laundered cotton and linen covers will make tired and tatty upholstery look more wholesome. Neat, firm cushions and bolsters will pull together a saggy sofa, just as squashy ones soften up unforgiving upholstery.

art

A stunning piece of art, ceramic or sculpture will be the focus of attention and add zest to a simply furnished room. Suss out new talent at affordable prices at art school degree shows, art fairs and local galleries or be brave and hang your own creations, or those of your nearest and dearest. If you can't trust your judgement, then opt for good-quality reproductions of the finest art from galleries and museums.

wild life

Sometimes a joyful vase of flowers can do more for a room than any decorating scheme. Save money on paint and fixtures and fittings and invest instead in TLC and fresh flowers. Plants keep us in touch with nature and can calm an interior as well as the soul. A tank of fish will fulfil feng shui requirements and soothe overactive minds.

leather

Just as a beautiful, good-quality handbag or belt can make a chain-store suit look a million dollars, a single leather chair, footstool or even just a cushion will lend an impression of quality to a room. Keep to classic colours: tans, creams and dark browns all look expensive.

smart tricks wow!

a splash of colour

Your home may be perfectly pleasant, but perhaps lacks just a bit of character. If you fancy a change, why not go mad with colour? If your existing furniture and furnishings are plain and simple, go for something vivid. If you are feeling bold, paint the whole room – or the whole house – otherwise adopt the 'just one wall' strategy. Whatever you decide, go for a really outrageous colour.

collector's items

There's no need to hide your peculiar passions or apologise for any anorak tendencies. Bring out those quirky collections and display them with pride. Whether it is stamps, toy robots, beer mats or even shoes, a collection has the potential to be the centre of attention and add a touch of wow! to a dull room or more restrained environment.

family portrait

Commissioning a family portrait can be expensive, but is a great investment. If funds are low, you could always have a go yourself. Why not scan in a photograph and play around on a computer or photocopier to produce your own version of an Andy Warhol or a Julian Opie? Better still, equip your five-year-old with brushes, paint and a huge canvas to produce your very own brat-art.

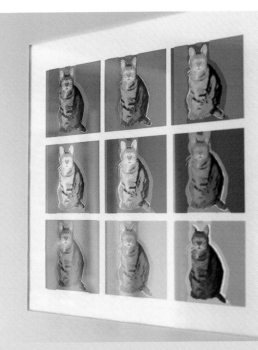

one-off

If you can't afford to furnish your whole house with the latest designs or most elegant antiques, invest in a single fine piece and make it the star attraction. Set off simple surroundings with a stunning chair, ornate mirror or extravagant bed. Put a curious piece of sculpture in the hall or custom-made stained glass in the smallest window. Indulge and enjoy.

smart tricks harmony

Whether you are putting together a home on a shoestring or simply saving money to spend on other things, as a thrifty homemaker you need to be on the lookout for cheap alternatives and bargains. A houseful of inexpensive or second-hand furniture can look a mess unless you impose some sort of order, but it is possible to create a sense of harmony, be it harmony of style, tone or spirit.

style, scale and proportion

Sticking to one design style to create an Arts and Crafts idyll or a Pop Art pad will naturally pull a room together, but be careful it doesn't look stilted, mannered or just plain boring. Cheap imitations of design classics often don't cut the mustard, either aesthetically or in terms of quality, so if your taste errs towards the distinctive, invest in the real thing, supplemented with simpler, plainer pieces.

One of the most obvious differences that distinguishes inexpensive furnishings from the expensive is scale. Economy solutions often use less material so proportions are not as generous, and budget buys can end up looking like the poor relations. For example, a cheap sofa or chest can look insignificant next to a more expensive model and detract from an otherwise attractive interior. Economy of scale applies not only to height, width and depth but also to the thickness of materials used and the size of detailing and fittings, such as knobs and handles.

materials and colour

Keeping things simple extends to the materials used for furniture, furnishings, fittings, floors, work surfaces and equipment. Raw materials, including unpainted wood and stone, and natural fibres, such as cotton, linen and wool, all have an intrinsically harmonious quality and so work well together to impart a calm feel in a room.

Using too many different materials will look messy, even if they are expensive, so obeying the rules of good design and keeping to a restricted palette is even more important for thrifty interiors.

matching up

Inconsistencies within colour and finish can spoil the overall effect of an otherwise good-looking selection of furniture. Wood finishes, particularly on new furniture, can vary widely in colour, which is just enough to make them look a mishmash rather than a carefully chosen collection.

Painting everything the same colour, or shades of one colour, will unify them but you can also try toning down the differences with a coat of finishing oil or liquid wax, which has a touch of stain in it. Use a limited collection of fabrics to cover a motley assortment of upholstery and make them look as if they belong together, but avoid an over-conscious, over-co-ordinated look by choosing a selection of tones, textures and perhaps a smattering of pattern.

spirit

There is much to be said for a lived-in look as long as it points to a relatively harmonious life rather than conflict. A plethora of books and objects and a crowd of furniture can still evoke the spirit of harmony in a happy, cheerful household where imposing an air of elegance and even opulence may be a matter of imaginative arrangements, evidence of tender loving care or a vase of fresh flowers.

thrifty looks economy modern

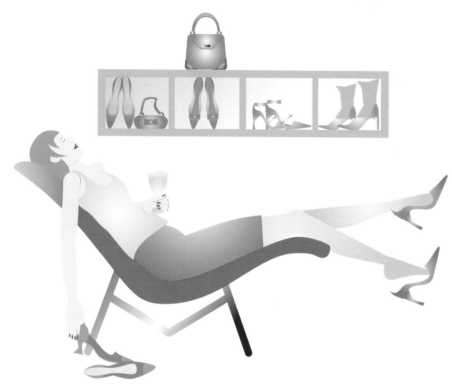

unless your only activity is quiet meditation and you eat out all the time, you will have a fair amount of stuff to house. Storage is, therefore, an important consideration in order to keep possessions, equipment, clothes and sundry bits and bobs under control, and preferably under cover. Discretion and discipline are the buzzwords so put only good-looking objects on display. For everything else, think cupboards with plain fronts that look like part of the wall and melt into the background.

For those who want modern to demonstrate their fashion credentials it is possible to do it with accessories. It doesn't have to be expensive, huge or a big statement, it can be something as small and discreet as a single cushion, vase or picture. Alternatively, you could just casually drape a designer cardigan over the back of a chair, or use your new shoes or handbag as ornaments.

Successful modern looks chic and expensive and economy modern can be cooked up from inexpensive ingredients picked off the shelves of the large furniture superstores, used sparingly and carefully arranged in a crisp, clean setting.

The dictionary definition of 'modern' refers to 'of the present or recent times' and 'fashionable', so in theory, any current design trend can be said to be modern. However, the traditional concept of modern is of simple shapes, clean lines and pared-down interiors with little or no decoration. The minimalist vision of the perfect white box used to be strictly for architects and purists, but constant exposure in magazines and TV programmes following homeowners in pursuit of a 'light and airy' space has brought it a

wider audience. However, this form of modernism is extreme and some people are reacting against it in favour of a more comfortable and characterful look that includes colour, curves, pattern and texture. This shift can be seen in the recent revival and reappraisal of the Scandinavian style, which, with richly coloured wood and geometric patterns, has brought in a warmer, less clinical look.

Modern is now synonymous with 'uncluttered'. Thrifty modernists are well advised to keep things simple, but

10 modern issues

keep it simple
Don't overcrowd a room and don't use too many different styles and designs. Stick to simple geometric shapes – the odd gentle curve is permissible but absolutely no twiddly decorative trims.

illusion of space
For the must-have, 'light and airy' feel, use light colours and choose furniture that is raised above the ground on legs or castors.

hidden storage
Clear away the clutter and invest in smart built-in storage. Narrow, full-height doors with no horizontal lines to break up the space are very architectural and will also make a low-ceilinged room look and feel higher.

size matters
Keep a sense of proportion and think horizontally. A hotchpotch of different heights will not give you those desirable clean lines.

bare minimum
Keep floors and walls plain. Bare wooden, stone or tiled floors are great, so is rubber but it is expensive. Paint imperfect floors or cover with plain carpet and rugs.

set the scene
Less furniture looks best, but as it focuses attention on the background, invest money in getting walls, floors and woodwork into tip-top condition.

colour intensity
Control those colours and restrict that palette. Avoid cheap-looking, bright colours and finishes and go for the sophisticated and subtle.

bare necessities
Keep windows bare if possible but, if the view, privacy or cold is an issue, use blinds, shutters, fabric panels or straight, unfussy curtains.

define and refine
For the crisp look, choose materials such as stainless steel, aluminium, glass, plastics, laminates and smooth wood with a subtle grain.

see the light
Pay attention to lighting. There are plenty of smart, simple and surprisingly inexpensive light fittings around – aluminium and frosted glass are perfect for modern.

thrifty looks delightful dilapidation

Nowadays, second-hand doesn't necessarily mean second rate, especially now that the lived-in look is a fashion statement. Perhaps it is because we live in a fast-track, impersonal age that we currently appreciate old things and find delight in dilapidation. Shabby furniture, peeling walls and chipped paintwork appear in various guises ranging from romantic rustic to remembered retro.

Many people enjoy seeing evidence of a past life in an object, believing it adds personality and makes it more precious. This approach is the ultimate in thrifty style as it encourages you to appreciate your possessions for what they are, rather than what you think they should be, and saves the unnecessary expense of doing things up or buying new.

Over time, garish colours can fade into sophistication and a bit of battering can be character building, but shabby chic isn't always quite as simple as it may appear. It requires a disciplined and dispassionate eye to distinguish between the potentially delightful and the downright disgusting.

A few rules apply. If something is of good quality and good design, it will probably maintain its dignity when in poor repair. Age rarely gives beauty to something cheap and nasty or inherently horrible. Cleanliness is also important. Freshly laundered threadbare fabrics are soft and charming, but a tatty sofa or rug can lose its charm if it is accompanied by anything sticky or crusty. The same goes for chipped paintwork, which can only look good if it is given a thorough wash.

It takes flair and a certain amount of courage to go all the way with the distressed look. You'll always have the odd visitor who asks when you are going to get round to decorating, but as long as you maintain order with fewer objects and a willingness to keep things clean and tidy it is a good option. The uncluttered look works best. Battered objects look more convincing against a freshly painted background and, similarly, if you love your distressed walls, keep the competition to a minimum with fewer, simpler furnishings.

For really small budgets, scrubbed floorboards are infinitely preferable to a hideous carpet, and stripped, washed-down walls much better than nasty wallpaper. When it comes to buying old or antique furnishings and accessories, something in pristine condition may be well beyond your pocket but something in not quite tip-top condition could well be affordable. Assess the damage not only for aesthetic qualities but for practical reasons: an old armchair may look just the thing but if the springs have gone it will be uncomfortable and possibly unusable. Repairs can be expensive and fiddly, some may even need the attention of an expert, but sometimes patience and basic DIY skills are enough.

Contrast can enhance the charm of the old and the pleasing purity of the new. A coat of paint will smarten up and cover up a certain amount of damage without destroying the character of an old table or chest of drawers, while new seat cushions and covers will make a sofa more comfortable as well as more attractive.

Of course, if is possible to make new look old by using special paint techniques or just by using old fabrics and coverings and traditional colours and finishes on furnishings, walls and floors. Many new products are now available ready distressed. Some are very successful but some are not, so be discriminating and make sure the dilapidation is definitely delightful.

shabby favourites

Old woollen, checked blankets – look for grungy browns, muted pinks and greens. Honeycomb and tapestry blankets, much favoured in the 1960s and sold in craft shops and woollen mills, are also back in favour.

Crochet blankets, shawls and cushions – charming and cosy. Watch out for tea cosies, too.

Old patchwork and quilted bedcovers – the more faded the better and don't worry if the insides are poking through.

Candlewick bedspreads – once considered completely naff but now definitely 'now'.

Big, saggy armchairs (just one, though, as more can look too scruffy). Leather is special but becoming hard to find at affordable prices.

Faded chintz – keep an eye open for old curtains, sofa and chair covers.

Metal garden furniture, wirework plant holders and bits and bobs. A bit of rust adds character.

Small, painted bookcases and shelves – a nostalgic alternative to smart shelving.

Faded pictures in stout wooden frames, including old sepia photographs (adopt your own ancestors).

thrifty looks natural calm

For many, the discipline of modernism is very appealing, but it just doesn't suit their lifestyle. However, a comfortable and a more casual environment can still look and feel calm, and applying a few principles of Zen will help. Space, simplicity, order, balance and harmony are important ingredients, as is a focus on nature.

Though not strictly minimalist, a Zen interior contains only items that are pleasing to the eye and practical. This is a useful rule for decluttering exercises, but as it does not preclude anything a bit battered or slightly out-of date, it is a philosophy that will appeal to the thrifty. Pleasing to the eye doesn't have to mean design perfect, so the imperfections of much-loved, familiar items are unimportant because their comforting presence is calming and good for the spirit.

An over-crowded room will seldom feel calm, so consider the space and leave enough room for moving around and stretching out. Though it may not always be possible to impose calm on family rooms, the philosophy is ideal for bedrooms where it is acknowledged that we sleep and relax better in an uncluttered environment: the cell-like simplicity of bare floors and walls, the minimum amount of furniture, just a comfortable bed, a bedside table and a few favourite items.

The chemical-rich, highly charged atmosphere of the technological age is at odds with our origins and it is not surprising that many are leaving the towns and opting for country living. Of those left behind, many more aspire to a simpler life and the beneficial effects of the countryside, including the appreciation of nature. Surrounding ourselves with colours and materials directly derived from nature can help us to re-connect and so become more relaxed and re-energised. Wooden and stone floors are perfect but wool carpet or natural fibre floor coverings will provide a quieter environment.

Along with colour and style, use some of the harmony smart tricks to induce an aura of calm with natural tones. Choose vegetable dyes rather than the harsher chemical varieties, solid woods and shapes that are rounded rather than sharp. Keep it serene by staying simple, with not too much to distract the eye or the brain. Calm doesn't necessarily mean stilted. Taking pleasure in the rituals of everyday actions such as cooking and cleaning is also a tenet of Zen and involves enjoying the beauty of everyday objects such as wooden bowls, simple white ceramics, even a favourite knife and chopping board.

Light is essential for wellbeing but a calm atmosphere is created through quality of light, whether it is filtering it through fine cotton or wooden slatted blinds or arranging lamps to provide pools of light, rather than illumination.

Colours in nature harmonise naturally. For inspiration think of your favourite places to create your own colour scheme. From the beach think of pebble and driftwood greys, sea blues and greens plus the warm colours of sand and shingle. Woods and forests contain mossy and pale leaf greens, loamy browns and seasonal splashes of brilliant bluebells. The landscape offers myriad shades of green fields and hedgerows including the sharp green of spring grass and early shoots, the fuzzy greens of hayfields, and meadows blotched with wild flowers. Mountains provide the textured grey of bare rock, stones and scrunchy scree, orange lichen, yellow broom, gentle heather purples, bracken browns and fern greens. Down in the orchard and vegetable plot, apples, pears, gooseberries and plums are enriched with the deeper tones of raspberries strawberries, red and blackcurrants. Add to the basket milky orange carrots, aubergine, pea green,and the speckled browns and purples of beans for a marvellously mellow palette.

This pretty cupboard is a new, inexpensive purchase from a large furniture store. For a softer look, the dark stain has been painted over with a primer, followed by eggshell.

The same pale colour has been used on the walls, free-standing cupboards and built-in cupboard doors. As well as being a restful shade for a bedroom, it provides a good background for the bright colours of the printed bedlinen and whimsical string of lights.

thrifty looks prudent panache

Cutting back on costs doesn't mean lowering your standards. Clever, thrifty people use flair instead of money to bring class, glamour and style to the humblest of homes. A throwaway gesture such as a scarf tied in the latest manner is all a stylish girl-about-town needs to prove she is on the fashion ball. And with a good hairdo and a wardrobe of carefully chosen basics in well-cut shapes that she knows flatter her good points and play down the not-so-good, she will always look and feel good. By adding carefully sourced extras from chain stores or charity shops, she can create a range of looks to suit personal taste and any occasion. Employing similar techniques, it is also possible to create an interior that is classy, snazzy, swanky or distinctly modish – not only easy on the eye, but easy on the pocket.

Perhaps you already have a house full of perfectly nice, good-quality stuff but it lacks a certain something – a dash of panache, in fact. It may be that all that is needed is a sensational wall colour or a good clean. Don't rush to throw things out or buy new; cast a critical eye over what you have and pick out the best.

A small but perfectly put-together collection of good-quality, well-designed furnishings is a good foundation for any style. With a few prudent purchases and a dash of panache – which is free – you can create a classy splendour. Attention to detail is the key whether it's exactly the right colour, the perfect doorknob or a witty dash of the unexpected. Making the best of what you've got – and showing it at its best, involves imaginative and unusual arrangements, clever accessorising, together with a well-groomed, cared-for look.

Panache is often all that's required to create a convincing impression of any style. It can turn traditional terrace into Jane Austen Georgian by setting pretty sofas, chairs, beds and chaise longues in sparsely furnished rooms painted in subdued beiges, greys, grey-greens and blues with scattered thin mats on bare floors. Eschewing modern units and fittings in favour of a capacious cupboard and a stone sink will keep up the pretence in any kitchen. Likewise, throw a large cloth over a nondescript table and place it centre stage, ready for afternoon tea or an hour's embroidery. And don't

forget that a little of what you fancy can do you and your home some good. The perfect antidote to minimal is a little bit of French. Indulge in discreet decoration, but don't feel guilty about gilt. Do keep it under control, though. A single gilt mirror is fine, but any more and you risk blowing your cover. With a little wit and wisdom and a lot of rubbing down and applications of wire wool, it is possible to transform quite vulgar repro, cheap French-style furniture complete with curvaceous legs, decorative carving and touches of gold into convincing pastiches of the real thing. Buy pretty shapes and paint them the colours of sugared almonds.

Arranging furniture with panache can make small rooms seem large, large spaces feel intimate and ordinary furniture appear special. After a good wax or a coat of paint, a small, junk-shop table can become a pretty writing desk or, with a couple of chairs and a candle, an intimate dining area.

Panache involves an approach to interiors that can enhance your lifestyle or suggest one that is more elegant, exciting or expensive than you can strictly afford.

thrifty looks bohemian

budget buys

Indulging in a little maximalism, which can be eclectic, ethnic, romantic or exotic, is the perfect way to achieve a big impact on a small budget. It is also a wonderful excuse to rebel against the de-cluttering police. Using throws, rugs and wall hangings in dangerously dark, rich colours and sumptuous fabrics with an adventurous spirit, you can create an interior to suit many moods and associations – from the excitement of the souk to the peace and seductive charm of the boudoir.

Brilliant for detracting from ugly surroundings and covering up shortcomings, it is also a relaxed alternative for those for whom dark and cosy is much more appealing than light and airy. Pile on the dhurries and throws and no one need know that a truly horrible sofa or disgusting carpet lurks underneath those wonderful layers of exotic pattern and colour. However, don't get too carried away or you might end up with a rather too convincing imitation of a student bedroom or your very first bed-sit. The grown-up approach to bohemian is a little more discriminating and sophisticated with a sense of order imposed by pruning out the grubby, tacky or seriously tatty.

Variations on a bohemian theme include the happy, hippy look which is essentially bare and simple but with a sprinkling of Indian bedspreads, wall hangings, pretty glass lamps, big floor cushions and lots of candles. A spiced-up version features oriental carpets, rugs, kelims, dhurries, rich embroideries, jewel coloured walls and fabrics plus a selection of ethnic objects including large pots, baskets and decorative, carved wooden beds, cupboards, tables and stools.

Alternative, arty people take their inspiration from Charleston farmhouse, home to Bloomsbury Group members the painters Duncan Grant and Vanessa Bell, who decorated walls, doors, floors, fireplaces, furniture and screens with exuberant patterns and figures. This thrifty way of turning the ordinary into the extraordinary can best be achieved by someone who possesses more than a dab of artistic talent. But even if you don't, you could use a stencil, and stick to something simple such as a table or the doors of a small cupboard.

Another opportunity for a little opulence is the boudoir – now making a comeback as a refuge for busy women where they can re-engage with their feminine side. Indulge in silks and satins, lace and velvet, fringed shawls and pretty furnishings, including chaises longues and glamorous dressing tables complete with stool and silver-backed hairbrushes.

indian cotton bedspreads
Plain and patterned, still to be found in ethnic shops and markets. Great for covering sofas, chairs, tables and beds and can also be used as curtains.

african prints
Scour markets and specialist shops for lengths of fantastically colourful printed fabric which can be used for everything from covers to curtains.

cotton dhurries and kelims
Plentiful in high streets, markets and warehouse stores. Some are quite small, so go for layers. Everything from bright, bold stripes to subtle traditional patterns suit a variety of moods and styles. OK on the floor but light colours soon look grubby. Good for covering furniture or hung at windows or on walls.

oriental-style carpets
Pseudo-oriental carpets from markets and bargain shops are sometimes thin. Choose the best colours and they can look convincing, especially when layered.

saris and embroidered fabrics
Shops in the less smart parts of town usually stock a selection of Moroccan-style fabrics. Use for covers, cushions, wall hangings and pure decoration. Take advantage of the colours and rich embroideries of traditional sari lengths, which make fabulous curtains or hangings round a bed.

make the most
of what you've got

In our eagerness to create a new look or way of living, it is easy to overlook the good points of what we've already got. It is also easy to believe that nothing short of a daring architectural scheme or a complete refit will bring our home up to the high standards we are now led to expect. Such schemes are expensive and, though they can be a worthwhile investment, making the most of what you've got can be a less stressful and more thrifty way of going about things.

the big picture

Unless your home is derelict or in a bad state of repair, think twice before embarking on the expense and hassle of building works, architects and building regulations, to say nothing of the stress of 'having the builders in'. There is no denying the appeal of huge spaces with acres of glass, but there is also no point denying that achieving it costs money.

You may well decide that invest is best, and major improvements will not only provide the much-needed extra space or better use of what you've already got, but also increase the value of your property. If you don't have the dosh, don't despair. A lack of funds doesn't have to mean a lack of style.

Take a holistic approach to your house, flat or apartment and apply the practical and thrifty approach to home improvements, which makes the most of what's already there. Removing dirt, dreadful decoration and damaged or unnecessary fixtures and fittings will reveal its good points, and you may be pleasantly surprised to find that a relatively inexpensive programme of repairs, rearranging the space and a cheering coat of paint will produce the home you've always wanted and didn't know you had.

open up

Knocking down walls may give you the loft look, but it can cost a lot both in terms of work and, if you are not careful, a reduction in the value of your property. Increasingly, people are putting walls back as the pleasures of large space, open-plan living become less attractive when it comes to privacy, heating and noise, especially if you have a family.

You may, however, still hanker for the light and airy look and there are less drastic, and less expensive, ways of achieving it. Just removing the doors between the kitchen, hall and living areas will make a difference. If this is likely to bring about an unacceptable level of noise or a problem with cooking smells, then think carefully, but even propping doors open semi-permanently will create an impression of more space. If you open up other areas to permanent view, you will maximise the illusion of one big space, particularly if you continue the same decorative scheme throughout all the rooms. One of the most effective ways of doing this is by restricting yourself to one floor finish and one wall colour and using this throughout the space so that the rooms appear to flow into one another.

knock through

While the thrifty approach may preclude major building works, knocking down one wall is relatively easy and not very expensive. Most people opt to increase the size of a kitchen or living area by knocking through into adjacent rooms, sometimes opening up the space completely to provide one large area for cooking, dining and living.

Alternatively, you could also consider knocking through into a hallway – a space that is often underused and may have windows that will bring in extra light. It does, however, mean being open to the stairs and bedrooms, so again before making a decision, consider whether there may be any noise or smell pollution problems. This works particularly well if you have an entrance porch; if not, then make provision for draught-proofing the front door during the cooler months.

glaze over

The main attraction of large spaces is that they are, or appear to be, full of light. A cheaper alternative to removing walls is to replace solid doors with glass-panelled ones, which are readily available at DIY stores and relatively inexpensive.

Replacing a window with glass-panelled French doors is not too much trouble and will make a room not only

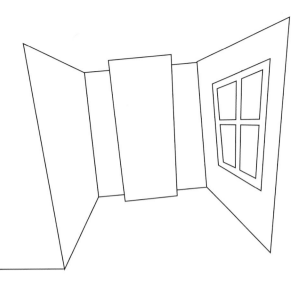

lighter but more elegant. For a dramatic effect, replace a whole wall with large patio doors. This will be more expensive as it entails putting in supporting beams and employing experts, but even so it's not hugely expensive for the impact that it will give.

If you can't afford a conservatory, consider a lean-to greenhouse – they are often reasonably priced and there is no law saying you have to use them exclusively for plants.

rethink your space

If moving house or getting in an architect are simply not viable options, it is possible to achieve amazing results by just changing how you allocate and utilise your space. Consider turning your house upside down by moving living areas upstairs and bedrooms downstairs. This will make the most of the upstairs space, views and sunshine during the daytime. If you crave privacy, a small, seldom-used boxroom could double as a private retreat, and a generous bedroom could provide a sitting area that is out of bounds to the rest of the household. Make the most of any nooks and

crannies, especially the space under the stairs that is usually given over to storage but could successfully be made into a cloakroom or shower room, opened up and fitted out as a work area or used as extra seating-cum-spare bed.

We all know that rooms with less clutter look bigger. Although a wall of purpose-built cupboards may take up a reasonable slice of your room, they will accommodate huge amounts of stuff and equipment. In a kitchen, large cupboards can house everything, including washing machines and dishwashers. The benefits of proper storage for clothes are obvious; likewise, a heap of toys or even a whole office can be hidden away in the evenings to free up the room for more restful or recreational activities.

Loft conversions can be a lot cheaper than moving house, as well as adding value to the existing one, but it is certainly not a cheap option and needs to be done by a professional who will ensure that work is carried out properly and complies with any building regulations. Don't forget to consult your neighbours; you may need permission

from them to carry out any work on party walls. Before you get too excited, make sure there is room for a proper staircase – a pull-down or rope version is OK for infrequent visits, but is no good for regular use. For rooms with sloping ceilings, a dormer window can increase the usable space but beware the planning regulations and think carefully how it will look from the outside. A badly designed scheme will not only look horrible, it can seriously affect the value of your home.

If you've really run out of room indoors but have spare space outdoors, get a shed. A small shed can take the pressure off indoor storage and even a modest-sized version can act as summer house, playhouse, studio, office or bolt hole.

a coat of paint

Paint is eminently affordable, making it possible to perform miracles of transformation for a surprisingly small sum.

walls and woodwork

A coat of paint provides you with the proverbial 'blank canvas' upon which to create your own picture of domestic life. Any house can be made brighter and better if it is painted throughout in white or a pale neutral colour with the added advantage that it will look and feel bigger – particularly good for small houses or rooms.

For a plain or relatively characterless house you will find that its shortcomings are less obvious with careful use of paint – unattractive features can be painted into the background by using the same colour for walls and paintwork. Paint over rough, damaged or patchy surfaces and you will find that imperfections become virtually invisible, especially when your possessions are in place.

For characterful and architecturally beautiful homes, a coat of paint emphasises good points and pleasing proportions and allows distinguishing features to stand out. Pick out quality woodwork in super glossy or muted matt paint in toning or contrasting colours.

floors

Bare floors are all the rage. If you have floorboards that are in good condition, it is relatively easy and inexpensive to strip them and turn them into a fashionable feature. If the boards are a bit rough, give them a good coating of floor paint which is hard-wearing and now available in many of the trendy colours.

Better-quality boards can take the more subtle watercolour approach, using washes of emulsion sealed with a robust matt varnish or waxed and allowed to acquire the well-worn look. Use light colours, especially if the room is small or dark. Dark or bright colours can look great but could become oppressive and drive you mad after a while. Do a good job – prepare well and paint carefully.

furniture

A coat of paint covers up dull, dirty or damaged wood and old paint. It's a well-known fact that painting a jumble of odd chairs the same colour will create a quirky but matching set; but, equally, a set of ordinary chairs can be enlivened by painting them different colours. Whether they are old or new, prosaic or characterful, tables, cupboards, chests of drawers, storage chests and trunks, bookcases and shelves can all be transformed and rehabilitated with a coat of paint. A thick coating of white gloss paint disciplines even the scruffiest piece of furniture, while dull matt can add sophistication. Convert starkly new into convincingly old using simple but effective paint effects.

fittings

Built-in wardrobes, cupboards and shelves are useful but not always very attractive or interesting. You can, however, minimise or maximise their impact with a coat of paint. Use the same colour as the walls if you want them to blend into the background, but for a bit of fun turn them into a feature with colour.

In this small house, the use of a single colour on the walls, furniture and fittings unifies the space, making it seem much larger and maximising the light.

Any room can look bright, clean and beautiful after a liberal application of white or very pale paint. Hard-wearing gloss paint accentuates the good points of a piece of furniture or woodwork and, as well as protecting it, it can be easily wiped clean.

style check fashion update

Before consigning your possessions to the charity collection or car boot sale, take another look. It's easy to take things for granted and to hang on to old prejudices regarding style. Fashions change and designs that were once consigned to the back of the cupboard may now be the height of chic, so take a second look and you may find a treasure trove of things you didn't know you liked.

fancy china

Tea sets and dinner services evoke a more formal and leisurely approach to dining. For thrifty people, for whom eating in is the new eating out, taking tea and dining formally are not only a great antidote to fast food and fast living but an opportunity to appreciate good food. Cheer up new plain ceramics by mixing in a few pretty florals.

lamps

Modern lighting design is sleek and functional and much of it is very inexpensive. But don't dismiss old lamp bases or standard lamps as they can be given a new lease of life with a plain drum shade, and some even look OK with just a bare bulb, especially as there are lots of new shapes to choose from. However, old-fashioned shades look quirky and friendly, so why not hang on to them.

dining suites

Dining suites are sometimes thrown out as something old-fashioned, but give them a second chance. A good-sized table and set of chairs in a kitchen or sitting room may inspire 'proper' family mealtimes, and one of the best way of entertaining friends is round a table full of good food and wine. The dining-room table also provides space for homework, sewing and other homely pursuits.

sideboards

Sideboards are back in favour as they are incredibly useful. Traditionally a home for table linens, drinks and glasses, they still perform that function very well but are also good for CDs, DVDs and even sound systems. Learn to appreciate the solid wood versions from the 1930s and '40s, the lighter more idiosyncratic shapes from the 1950s and the long low ones from the 1960s and '70s.

Hide an ugly frame and make reading in bed more comfortable with a quilt draped over the bedhead. Old ones look special, but there are plenty of pretty new ones at reasonable prices.

As well as rejuvenating the bed frame, cover dodgy springs with wooden slats and replace saggy old mattresses with new. Complete the rehabilitation by investing in new pillows and duvets and bedlinen from widely available, ever-expanding, good-quality but modestly priced ranges.

reuse and recycle

Rather than throwing furniture out because it is unattractive, or perhaps it doesn't quite perform the right function, use a little creative imagination to see whether you can use it in a different context or guise. A bit of re-invention can turn an item into a useful, smart and even special piece of furniture.

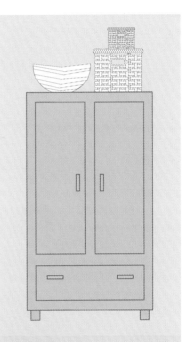

dressing table

The humble dressing table, deemed old-fashioned and outmoded, was discarded in favour of more cupboard space. But recently they have been sneaking back into fashion, along with the penchant for glamour and dressing up. Reconfigure and rejuvenate them with a coat of paint in a brilliant, unexpected colour. If necessary, remove any damaged or really ugly mirrors, mouldings, knobs and handles and replace them with new or funky alternatives.

chest of drawers and dressers

If you've got your clothes storage sorted and find you have a spare chest of drawers, it could be given a new lease of life in the kitchen. The drawers of a chest can be used for anything from table linen to packets of rice. Hang an inexpensive shelf unit above it, paint them both the same colour and you have an instant kitchen dresser – a place to store and show off your best china.

wardrobe

Don't hide your hallway under a pile of coats, bags and shoes. Store everything in that wardrobe you were about to throw out. If there are shelves for scarves, hats and other accessories, so much the better. Alternatively, hang one of those canvas pockets inside for just such a purpose. Use the space on top for storage, perhaps with a colourful basket for seasonal accessories.

good housekeeping clean it up

When a home is looking tired and scruffy, it's too easy to think that nothing short of a complete makeover will bring it back to life. We often take our surroundings for granted, seeing only the dull finishes, stains, tatty edges and general lacklustre appearance rather than appreciating the good properties and personalities of our homes. We all know how a room responds to a quick tidy and a bit of fresh air, so think what a thorough wash and brush-up could do.

Cleaning has been described as the new sex. This may be stretching a point, but there is no doubt that good housekeeping has gained a higher profile in recent years. Some of the most popular visitor events at big country houses are the 'below stairs' activities, including spring cleaning and the care of textiles, furniture and precious objects. Instead of a makeover that will cost money and involve decisions about new schemes, why not adopt a stately home attitude and give your space a healthy dose of TLC. This is not only the cheaper option but a thrifty one too as it will ensure that your furniture and furnishings last longer.

a good clean

Start at the top of your house or apartment equivalent so that you are not passing through already cleaned areas to get to the unclean. Take down any curtains and remove loose covers from sofas, chairs and cushions. Take down blinds and any other window coverings so that you can give the window a thorough clean.

Launder any washable fabrics using a gentle detergent. It is not necessary to dry-clean heavy curtains or covers every year, so if they have been cleaned in the recent past, just give them a good vacuum using the narrow nozzle to get down the sides and backs of chairs and sofas. Treat any marks with a stain remover.

Wash, dry-clean or vacuum Roman blinds. Plastic or metal slatted blinds can be washed in the bath or under the shower using mild detergent or spray cleaners. Wooden slatted blinds should be dusted or wiped with a damp cloth (do this before taking them down as it is easier to do this in situ).

Get rid of the dust from all surfaces using a vacuum cleaner, including floors, walls, ceilings and doors. Make sure you get into all corners and mouldings. Use the small nozzle of the vacuum cleaner along the edges between the skirting board and floor.

It's not necessary to wash walls (it is easier and more fun to repaint them) but obvious dirt and stains around light switches or areas of heavy traffic can be removed with mild detergent. However, you might end up with an obvious clean patch so it may be best to wash the whole wall or repaint. Instead of fully repainting it is possible to freshen up emulsion with watered-down paint (approximately one part paint to two parts water). Apply with paintbrush rather than a roller.

Wash all woodwork using a soft scouring sponge for excess goo, but don't scrub too hard as you will destroy the surface and encourage more dirt. Dry with soft, cotton cloths (tea towels are good).

Vacuum carpets thoroughly and shampoo if really necessary. Try not to do this too often as it destroys some of the stain retardants and natural properties of the fibres so that carpets then get dirty more quickly. Waxed or oiled wooden floors should be repolished or oiled. Wash varnished floors with a damp mop or cloth and apply another coat of varnish if the surface shows bad signs of wear. Painted floors can be mopped using mild detergent and should be repainted or resealed if in a bad state. Use soap rather than detergent to wash stone floors. Ceramic tiles and vinyl will always benefit from a good scrub.

spring clean sense

Protect yourself from splashes, bashes and harmful chemicals by wearing gloves, overalls and sensible shoes with the laces carefully fastened. Don't wear baggy trousers as you could trip over them. Always tie back long hair or wrap it up in a scarf.

Begin at the top of the house or the equivalent in a flat so that you are not passing through already-cleaned areas to get to the unclean. Start at the top of each room – ceilings first, floors last.

Protect and preserve – cover furniture and floors with dust sheets or polythene and protect vulnerable corners with old blankets.

First get rid of any dust from all surfaces (a vacuum cleaner is good for this). Dust turns to dirt when it comes into contact with water, so removing it reduces cleaning, particularly on surfaces that are to be washed down.

If cleaning really isn't your thing, consider getting in a professional company to do the job. Obviously it will cost more but it can be the thrifty option, especially if you have valuable furniture and furnishings or a high-quality flooring, such as wood block or stone, which needs careful treatment.

10 tools for janitor joy

dust sheets
Cover furniture to keep out dust and any splashes that could damage or stain surfaces and fabrics. A good way to put old sheets to use, but for precious items add extra protection in the form of plastic sheeting.

good-quality cotton cloths
Old sheets make good cloths, as cotton is better at serious cleaning than disposable wipes. Squeeze out for a non-smear finish, wash and reuse. Cotton dusters don't leave fluff behind and can be laundered.

specialist products
Although often expensive, specialist cleaners can give good results. Before buying, read the label to check it is the right product for the job – using the wrong cleaner can seriously damage materials and surfaces.

feather dusters
Gentle but efficient. Particularly good for cleaning books and precious items that get very dusty. Long-handled versions deal with fine cobwebs, but long-handled brushes may be better for the larger, spookier variety.

sponges and scourers
Good for stubborn stains and dirty deposits. Use gentler, non-stick pan sponges for delicate surfaces. Nylon scourers are great dirtbusters for all jobs, from preparing paintwork to scrubbing down wooden furniture.

eco cleaning
White vinegar is the new star of the cleaning department. It is highly effective in removing grease, limescale and soap deposits. Mixed with bicarbonate of soda, white vinegar makes an effective surface cleaner.

mops, brooms and brushes
Soft brooms get fine dust and debris out from corners and along skirting boards. A dustpan and brush is an essential companion to the broom, but a short-handled brush is useful for awkward corners and stairs.

vacuum cleaner
The only efficacious way to get dust out of carpets, curtains, upholstery and beds. Good for bare floors, too. Buy one with a good set of tools for cleaning corners and crannies. Don't forget to empty the bag frequently!

stepladder
Don't risk life and limb balancing on makeshift or rickety ladders. Lightweight aluminium stepladders are inexpensive, easy to move around and provide a safe way of reaching ceilings, tops of walls and windows.

mild detergent and bleach
Mild detergent is sufficient for general cleaning, including windows. Gentle household soap suits delicate surfaces, while bleach is an efficient germ-killer, with whitening and stain-removing powers. Dilute and use sparingly.

instant freshen-ups

fresh air and ventilation

Just one exhaled breath on a window pane or mirror creates mist and smears, Multiply that by the thousands of breaths you take every day, then add in the steam from baths, showers, cooking, washing up and laundry and you begin to understand the importance of good ventilation. Consider also the number of germs set free in day-to-day life, plus the chemicals and pollutants released by cleaning materials, cosmetics and beauty products, then add in the chemicals present in carpets, fabrics, paints and building materials, and chances are it won't be long before you get the urge to open a window.

We are, however, encouraged to conserve the expensive and potential planet-harming energy we all use in heating our homes by insulating, sealing up holes and making sure windows and doors are draught-free. Add to this our (often necessary) obsession with security and you end up living in a hermetically sealed environment with poor air circulation, which affects our health and that of our home and its contents. The results of poor ventilation include condensation, mould, mildew, stuffiness and unpleasant smells.

smelling sweet

A fresh-smelling, well-ventilated home will make you feel healthier and more alert, but avoid using artificial deodorisers or room scents as many of them contain a cocktail of chemicals that mask smells by manipulating your olfactory senses. Keep things natural and stick to scented plants, flowers, candles and oils.

A few drops of essential oil in water heated over a flame in a ceramic oil-burner will scent the air and set a mood. Investigate the properties of various oils. Lavender is known for its relaxing properties, whereas rosemary is a good pep-you-up. A specialist can create a formula to suit your personality and requirements. Only use scented candles if you can afford the good ones with natural ingredients, don't even think about buying the cheap ones as their smells will almost certainly be chemically based and will pollute rather than clear the air.

A vase of flowers cheers up the grimmest room and if they are scented then all the better. Go for subtle rather than pungent perfumes and opt for seasonal blooms to harmonise with body rhythms and enhance wellbeing. Roses smell best in summer, narcissi enhance the freshness of spring and winter jasmine raises the spirits. If you have a garden or even a window box, select plants for their scent which, wafted in through an open window is the best room freshener of all.

thrifty consumer

Conspicuous consumption is so last year. Nonetheless, thrifty people with shopaholic tendencies don't have to miss out on their favourite pastime. In fact, a nose for a bargain, an instinct for what is likely to be the next big thing plus a willingness to spend hours in pursuit of the perfect purchase are great assets as long as they are accompanied by self-control, a clear idea of what you are looking for, an ability to say no and the patience to wait for what you really want.

buying old where to shop

Antiques are expectedly pricey. Second-hand used to mean cheap until 'retro' became big business; competition and prices are escalating. The plethora of TV programmes inflating the value of anything old from a bureau to a biscuit tin has also raised the stakes, so sellers are less likely to let things go for a song. Getting real bargains is becoming more difficult, but a keen eye and an ability to see beyond any shortcomings can still bring rewards, as well as being good fun.

antique and vintage dealers

There is a perception that genuine antiques are very expensive, but prices often compare favourably with the high end of new and the rising cost of 'retro'. While rare antiques or examples of fine craftsmanship will be costly, the plainer, more solid stuff is often good value for money. Cultivate a friendship with local antique dealers to pick up useful tips. If you have a preference for particular styles and eras, they will keep an eye open for fine examples at good prices for regular customers. The genuine article usually costs money, but sometimes it is worth it as you cannot rely on happenstance to pick up what you are looking for. Use these dealers to learn what to look out for so you will recognise a lucky bargain in charity shops, jumble and car boot sales.

antique fairs and markets

The posher antique fairs are held in exhibition centres, hotels and town halls, appeal to serious collectors and often involve serious money. The vendors are professionals so don't expect very low prices. More modest affairs held in streets, market places and village halls are more modestly priced. But in any market, prices can vary from genuine bargains to scandalously over-priced so knowledge is a fine thing. Research the market to get some idea of what to look out for and what is a fair price.

sales rooms

Look before you buy, examine the piece and make sure it is what you want. Prices vary depending on how trendy the item is and how many dealers are bidding. Remember, a dealer needs to sell his or her goods on at a much higher price, but a winning bid could still be below the market value. Visit a few sales before deciding to make a bid, then you'll get some idea of prices and what type of stuff is still cheap. Consider all of an item's good points and decide whether it is suitable for you or could be the next fashion. If you are willing to pay a good price for something you really want, make sure it is in good condition. Paying full whack for something you have to spend a lot of time and money putting right is not thrift sense.

flea markets

The distinction between antique and flea markets is blurred, but flea markets are usually held outdoors. Small town markets in less touristy or trendy areas are more likely to yield bargains. Markets in different countries offer a less familiar, and possibly more interesting, selection of goods.

salvage yards

Brilliant places for finding old doors, window frames, floorboards, mouldings, stone sinks, cast-iron baths and many unusual items of architectural interest. It can be expensive as this sort of stuff is in great demand, but may be worth the expense if you want to replace original fittings in properties where sensitive restoration is a worthwhile investment.

used office equipment suppliers

As well as desks, chairs and filing cabinets, you can also find tables and upholstered seating. Among the steel tubing and laminate (a good 'modern' material), you may find solid wood or metal desks, wooden plan chests and sometimes old filing systems and pigeon holes that make great storage. School chairs, lockers and cupboards offer good-quality design at reasonable prices.

internet shopping

Trading on the internet is increasing in popularity. It's not the same as poking around in dusty curiosity shops, but if you're after something special, you can search the whole world via the mouse. It's also a useful reference for checking the value of what you want to buy or sell. Use only reputable sites and exercise caution when paying for anything over the net. For private sales or purchases from smaller shops, make contact by telephone and ensure you have all the seller's details before making a payment.

second-hand and junk shops

Poking around in a crowded junk shop full of potential gems and bargains is, for many, one of life's great pleasures. Frequent visits are recommended to get the pick of any new stock. Look for the smaller items from house clearances, such as sets of table linen and china. Prices vary but they are the sort of places where you can make an offer.

charity shops

Once a great place for picking up cheap chic. However, some of the charities have now got their acts together and edit out the valuable stuff to sell at high prices or in their specialist shops.

car boot sales

Early visitors to car boot sales are the dealers and collectors, examining goods and making offers before the beleaguered seller has finished laying them out.

jumble sales

You stand a better chance of bagging a bargain at a jumble sale because the stuff isn't sorted beforehand: the jolly ladies in charge are not always tuned in to the latest design trends. The best buys are in affluent areas where the cast-offs are likely to be of good quality.

classified ads

Fun to read and you never know what might turn up.

skips

There are still exciting things lurking in skips, but you have get in there first. You have to be brazen enough to pillage in broad daylight in full view of passers-by. Chippendale chairs are rare finds, but furniture from the 1960s and '70s is not. Perfectly good rugs are often chucked out and it's worth looking in plastic bags for curtains and other textiles. Office furniture is another frequent skip dweller.

swap shop

The ultimate in thrift is either buying from the growing number of curtain and furniture exchanges and swapping or redistributing stuff among friends and family. Older people are often willing to swap or give away furniture or textiles they think are outdated, but that you know are trendy.

10 still-affordable things

hall stands
They add character to any hallway, as well as keeping coats, hats and umbrellas under control. Occasionally they are found in solid oak, but most often in dark wood which could look better painted. Some have a mirror.

rugs and mats
They can often be bought at giveaway prices. If they're a bit grubby, they may respond well to carpet shampoo. Threadbare is chic. Use several rugs in layers with the not-so-attractive ones at the bottom.

bed frames
Proper bed frames, especially wooden ones, are back in fashion. If the supporting base is missing, it is not too difficult to make a new slatted one from offcuts.

armchairs with wooden arms
There is a plentiful supply of smart armchairs, which are neither as big nor expensive as a fully upholstered chair so are good for small spaces. They are also easier and cheaper to freshen up with a tie-on chair cover.

small cupboards and units
Whether they are delightfully dilapidated or freshened up with a new coat of paint, you're bound to find a use for a pretty little cupboard or shelf. Hang wall units in twos and threes – they don't have to match.

door knobs and handles
It's not essential to have matching door knobs throughout your house, or even on a single piece of furniture. If you find something special, put it to good use.

lamp bases
Lamps are simple to update with a fashionable new shade, but they can also look good with just a bulb. Watch out for tall standard lamps.

wallpaper
Wallcoverings are back – and the older the better. Wallpaper you would have taken the stripper to only a few years ago suddenly looks great.

odd tiles
If you like the cosy, casual look and are feeling creative, a patchwork of tiles in a kitchen or bathroom can look great.

kitchen equipment
Keep an eye out for old storage tins, utensils, pots, pans, bread bins, cake tins, bread boards and cutlery.

buying old what to look out for

wardrobes and dressing tables

With more people than ever tuned in to the changing trends in interiors and the retro and vintage market, it is becoming harder to find real bargains. It is still possible, however, to pick up old wardrobes and dressing tables made from thin, not very nice wood with an unpleasant shiny varnished finish. These are still quite cheap so snap them up, put on a coat of primer to ensure that the paint will stick and give them a colour makeover using unexpected and brilliant shades. Reconfigure them by removing any damaged or really ugly mirrors, mouldings, knobs and handles and give them funky new replacements.

bureaus

Incredibly useful for keeping all the invoices, bills, passports, birth certificates and other paperwork that we all accumulate. A pull-down top provides space for a laptop computer or for writing good old-fashioned letters. Look beyond first impressions: if the finish is not very appealing, give it a coat of paint or stain.

utilitarian furniture

A lot of basic, solid furniture made in the 1930s and '40s is often overlooked because of its lack of distinguishing style details, but the quality of the materials and workmanship is high and the simple designs allow them to fit into most interiors. Made from mostly solid wood, it only needs a good clean and repolish or a coat of paint. Look for similar office, school and hospital furniture from the same period.

victoriana and edwardiana

Fashionable in the 1960s for those setting up home on a shoestring, the curvy, decorative and often large-scale furniture of the early 1900s was very popular. However, the fashion for minimal interiors has lessened its appeal so it should be possible to find a few bargains in the form of dining tables and chairs, large chiffoniers, armchairs and sofas. Look out for small delicate tables, cake stands, trays, odd bits of china, cutlery, cruet sets and pieces of silver.

picture frames and mirrors

There are still bargains to be had. Look especially for large, fancy picture frames and smarten them up or tone them down with paint. Seek out old, shaped mirrors usually hung by a chain, traditionally placed above a mantelpiece but equally at home in a bedroom or bathroom. They look fun when hung in twos and threes.

linens

Old cotton and linen is often thicker and softer than their new equivalents and prices can still be surprisingly low. As well as sheets and pillowcases, look for tablecloths, runners, napkins and antimacassars especially if they are hand-embroidered or edged in lace.

blankets, rugs and throws

With duvets now the bedding of choice, there are plenty of blankets lurking in junk shops, jumble sales and charity shops. Pick out any clean, good-quality woollen blankets and give them a good wash. You may be lucky and find old ones with fashionable stripes or window-pane checks, but the traditional cream or even pink blankets can look very good and cosy. Also, don't forget to take a second look at those candlewick bedspreads.

buying old best invest

Along with 'vintage', the term 'antique' is now used to describe any desirable and fashionable style from Hepplewhite to early Habitat. Encouraged by TV programmes that reveal the potential high value of our possessions, far more people are now in the know. This makes for a much more competitive market with higher prices, which is bad news for low budgets. However, sometimes it sound thrift sense to invest in good-quality pieces that will last for many years and appreciate in value. Here is a brief round-up of current popular styles.

late georgian

The elegance of Georgian architecture has inspired the interior fashion for panelled walls and doors, bare floorboards and woodwork painted in muted greens. Favoured furniture includes slightly shabby, deep armchairs, chaise longues and curvy-legged tables, just like those used by the upstairs aristocracy. But even more in demand is the stuff used by those below stairs, such as metal bed frames, large, solid cupboards and plain wooden chairs and tables, plus all manner of kitchen paraphernalia from stone sinks to oversized ceramic bowls and jugs. Original wooden panelling, floorboards, sinks, basins and other sanitary ware can be found in salvage yards, but expect to pay the going price.

arts and crafts

William Morris was the prime mover of this movement, whose ideals centred on quality materials and craftsmanship. Morris believed that you should 'have nothing in your home that you do not believe to be beautiful or useful'. Arts and Crafts furniture ranges from solid-looking cupboards, cabinets and settles, to more delicate, rush-seated chairs. Many of the original pieces were painted in dark colours and decorated with images. As it was handcrafted rather than mass-produced, examples by original members of the Arts and Crafts movement will be very expensive. However, the term is often applied to craftsman-made, solid, simple furniture from around the beginning of the twentieth century, the prices of which represent value for money compared to new pieces of comparative quality.

twentieth-century modern

This term is used to describe a wide range of modernist furniture from the design classics of the Bauhaus era to the more recent designs of the 1960s and '70s. Much of the furniture from these later periods has only just been rediscovered; things that were destined for skips a few years ago are now demanding eyebrow-raising prices. Unless they are in very poor condition, vintage pieces by Marcel Breuer, Le Corbusier and Charles and Ray Eames will be very pricey, as will originals by Scandinavian designers such as Alvar Aalto, Arne Jacobsen and Hans Wegner. Items by British designers Robin and Lucienne Day and Ernest Race are also keenly collected, as is the mass-produced, high-quality furniture from the 1950s to the 1980s made by companies such as Ercol and G-Plan. Knowing your styles and designers is essential: swatting up is recommended and there are plenty of reasonably priced, very good books on the subject. While you may not be able to afford some of the bigger pieces, console yourself with smaller items such as ceramics, glassware and textiles.

retro and nostalgia

There is a crossover with twentieth-century modern, but retro usually applies to anything reminiscent of the American 1940s and '50s diner look with lots of chrome, leather, plastics and bright colours. However, it also includes the 'suburban semi-detached' styles of the 1930s, '40s and early '50s, whose mass-produced furniture and furnishings have a comfortable, friendly, somewhat nostalgic look reminiscent of simpler times. Much is still affordable so look out for three-piece suites, dining and bedroom suites, enamel-topped tables, utility furniture, chintzy prints and patterned china.

late georgian panelled cupboard

late georgian scroll-armed sofa

arts and crafts dresser

art deco upholstered armchair

1950s modular storage unit

1950s lounge chair

1950s upholstered armchair

1960s pendant lamp

1960s seating system

buying old a word of caution

appliances

Modern appliances are efficient and safe, but with a few (mostly expensive) alternatives, their design tends to be hard-edged. Mostly they are available only in clinical white or stainless steel, which rather spoils the effect of a retro-style or lived-in look kitchen. For this reason, old fridges, cookers and ranges are very popular and, while some are fetching premium prices in specialist shops and on websites, it is still possible to pick up something for a lower price than a modern equivalent.

lighting

There are still lots of bargains to be had. Look for desk lamps, lamp bases and shades from the 1930s and '40s. Centre light fittings, often featuring coloured or patterned glass, were popular from the 1950s to '70s; once much reviled, they are now de rigueur. Chandeliers are also back in favour and odd pretty glass lamp shades can still be quite cheap. Check all plugs, cables and flexes and replace with new if they look at all dodgy. You can buy old-fashioned twisted flex for authenticity.

electrical goods

There are strict regulations regarding the sale of electrical goods, which are limited to licensed retailers. Electric fires and heaters are potentially the most dangerous appliances, so unless you know your way around electrics, leave them well alone. Your insurance company may refuse to pay up if they suspect dodgy, non-regulated equipment. As with lighting, check all cables and connections. Don't forget that foreign appliances are likely to be incompatible with the electricity supply.

cookers and ranges

A vintage cooker may perfectly complement your kitchen, but there are rules regarding safety. Any second-hand gas cooker being sold through a retailer is required by law to have gone through a series of safety checks. Any cooker, whether bought from a shop or through a private sale, must be installed by a registered CORGI fitter who will carry out the appropriate safety checks.

radiators

Cast-iron column radiators look great in old and modern environments alike. The real thing can be found in salvage yards and on the web. Though they look great, very often these radiators aren't terribly efficient, so get an expert to give them the once-over. Plumbing fitting sizes can make installing them more complicated. New versions are available which might, in the long run, be a better thrifty purchase.

woodworm

Check any wooden items for signs of live woodworm: fresh holes and deposits of sawdust are a reliable indication. For small items, it is relatively easy to treat the infestation using a proprietory product that can be either brushed on or squirted into the holes using a syringe. It may be wise to treat any troublesome item before bringing it into your home; that way, you won't allow the pests the run of the rest of your house.

buying new what to look out for

There was a time when good design and fashionable style were only available at the high, and expensive, end of the market. Today you can find both in a wide variety of places from the big out-of-town warehouses to high-street chains and bargain shops. Now that we are offered a huge selection of simple, good-looking furniture and fittings at remarkably low prices, 'cheap' has ceased to be a derogatory term. In fact, many low-cost items have become modern classics and can be found in the most gracious, as well as the most humble, homes.

Thrift isn't only about low prices; it also takes into account issues of value-for-money, suitability and sustainability. Buying for the short term may solve current budget deficiencies, but may turn out to have been a false economy if the goods need replacing soon after.

price control

When you buy something at the top end of the market, you pay more for style, quality and exclusivity. If you pay less, you may have to compromise on one or more of these.

It is now acknowledged that too much consumer choice causes stress and anxiety; faced with the profusion of products available for the home, it's easy to see why. Weighing up your options and balancing your budget can turn shopping into a far from relaxing activity, especially when the price of an item isn't always related to its quality or value.

Some stores specialise in a certain type of product and are therefore able to sell it cheaper, while larger retailers with greater spending power and bulk orders can also afford to keep prices low. It is possible therefore to find price variations within ranges of similar items.

Doing your homework, shopping around and examining the product in question will help identify the best value. A flexible attitude to budgets is also helpful. While thrifty people want, or need, to avoid high prices, it is always worth looking at the more expensive option as the difference in quality or style may be worth much more than the difference in price. For a fairly modest upgrade, you may get a far better buy.

basic instincts

As everyone buys clothes from large chain stores, wise shoppers know not to buy distinctive designs to avoid advertising exactly where you shop and meeting others similarly dressed. Smart shoppers buy the basics and then dress them up to create a style that is their own. This applies equally to interiors, where canny customers buy items that will be a discreet presence rather than a bold statement. Some department stores and high-street retailers may appear dated and dull, but look carefully at the merchandise as you may find a simple, inoffensive design that is of much higher quality, and better priced than its equivalent in a more trendy store.

long-lasting

As already stated, we live in a throw-away age, buying cheap items designed to last only a short time before being disposed of and replaced with new. Unfortunately, we are running out of room to dispose of all the rubbish, added to which it is a tremendous waste of precious resources and a threat to the environment. Buying less but spending more in the first place will not only help save the planet but will help you save money in the long run. For example, it may seem to make sense to buy an inexpensive sofa if it is going to be subjected to the ravages of children or pets, but a more expensive, better-quality item will be able to withstand such use and can be cleaned or re-covered over time.

lasting impression

Fashions come and go but classics stay the course. Spend money on quality and good, but simple designs that are capable of living through the fads and fancies of one era and obligingly fit in with the next. Remember also that it is often better to blow a whole budget on one or two good pieces as they will be the centre of attraction for now and the core of a collection for the future.

salesmanship

If you have champagne tastes but only a fizzy water budget, the sales are for you. Keep an eye on the smartest shops and make sure you know when their sales are on. Join their mailing list or check websites regularly for special offers, reductions, stock clearances or even closing-down sales. Most high-class stores have sale previews, so go along to see if it's worth packing the thermos and sandwiches ready to queue for a chance of getting your chosen bargain. As well as great sale reductions, shops often run a 10% or more discount offer on normal stock, which can make the previously unaffordable just about possible. Visit sales in their late stages when prices are further reduced. Anxious to get rid of stuff, the bargains are better and stores are open to offers.

quality control

The difficulty now is not finding something cheap, but knowing what to choose. Here are a few guidelines.

solid wood

Much of the cheapest furniture available is made from fibreboard, laminated with wood or plastic. While it looks okay, the edges are prone to damage. Solid wood look and wears better and can be treated with paint, stain or wax to improve its life expectancy.

dimensions

The success of a well-designed piece of furniture rests on its proportions and dimensions, as well as on the materials and styling. Cost cutting can sometimes lead to a less generous use of materials, which in the poorest examples results in a mean and cheap-looking product. Opt for designs that look robust, chunky rather than thin.

colour and finish

Inexpensive fabrics and laminates can look cheap in bright colours, so stick to whites and neutrals. Soft woods are sometimes given a coating of durable varnish to make them more hard-wearing, but it can look horrible. Paint or stain can cover such inadequacies.

safety in numbers

A cheap item on its own draws attention to itself, but gains confidence in a group. Inexpensive bookcases are remarkable value and look convincing when several are placed together.

best invest

The best modern design is elegant, seductive, perfectly formed, beautifully made and usually very expensive. If Modernism is your passion and only the best will do, the thrifty solution is to forego holidays, evenings out and a fully furnished house in order to purchase something special. A single item, such as a superb chair by Alvar Aalto, Hans Wegner or Ico Parisi or a piece of decorative glass by Tapio Wirkkala, is enough to add class and charisma to a whole interior. Just remember to keep the competition at bay and showcase your star turn in a simple, pared-down setting.

Original modern designs can increase in value, so as long as you look after them, they may be a good investment. If you are clever and can spot an up-and-coming designer, scour student degree shows and exhibitions for collectables of the future. You could even commission a piece made to your specifications.

Truly good design never dates; in fact it gets better with age. Investing in genuine design classics is always a good idea, but if you don't have the resources, there are plenty of good imitations around with the same clean lines and shapes. Mass production has led to a high level of quality at surprisingly low prices.

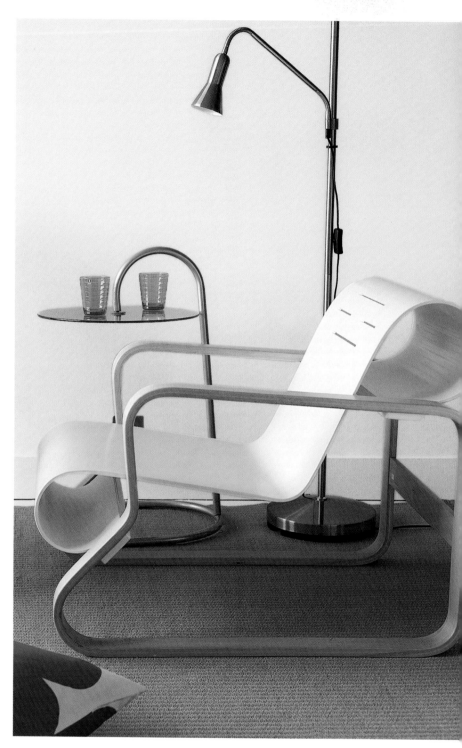

buying new cheapo classics

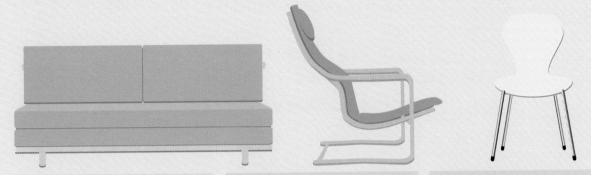

studio couch
Made up of square-edged cushions on a metal frame, this type of sofa is usually inexpensive. It looks smarter, and takes up less space, than a futon. It looks good left plain or softened with cushions and throws.

plywood frame armchair
Reminiscent of the designs of Marcel Breuer and Bruno Matthson, but the fact that it is not a direct copy makes this chair a classic in its own right. Very comfortable, especially with a matching footstool.

plywood dining chair
The popularity and versatility of Arne Jacobsen's Series 7 chairs have led to a number of imitations. Some are more blatant than others, but all possess an elegance and give the opportunity for a splash of colour.

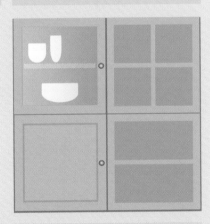

desk lamps
The best examples echo the workman-like shapes and proportions of the original angled desk lamp designed in 1934. They work equally well as table lamps, bedside lights, task lighting and, with special bases, floor lamps.

cafe furniture
Based on an original Spanish design, these chairs and tables are seen in coffee shops the world over. Cheaper versions are appearing in high-street chains. Perfect for outdoors, they also look good in a modern kitchen.

modular units
Some are a variation on the simple cube storage systems of the early 1960s, while others are more sophisticated modular units, poaching ideas from Jean Prouvé and Charles & Ray Eames.

5 good buys – low cost, high style

It's not only what you buy, but how you use it that turns inexpensive furniture into a stylish item. There are plenty of no-nonsense, cheap products around and they often work better if you use several together in a row or other formal arrangement. Keep things simple by choosing plain shapes and colours. Avoid anything that looks flimsy and don't mix too many different styles and materials.

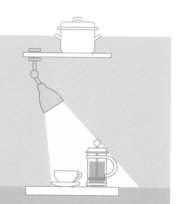

wooden boxes

DIY stores and large furniture chains sell a good selection of low-cost, stout, solid wooden-lidded boxes ready for staining or painting. They are, of course, great for storage, but can also become an attractive piece of furniture in their own right.

Not only do they provide ample hidden storage, but they can also double as a table, a seat or a useful surface for anything from the TV to a collection of precious objects. Several of these boxes placed side by side along a wall are a cheap alternative to modular storage, with the advantage that you can choose both the colour and finish.

clip-on lamps

Sophisticated lighting systems are expensive as they require a qualified specialist to install wires and fittings. Clip-on lamps are no trouble at all, needing only a nearby plug socket and a safe place where they can be securely clipped on. Use as task lights over a work surface or desk or as display lighting aimed at a picture or object. Turn towards the ceiling or wall to provide subtle background lighting.

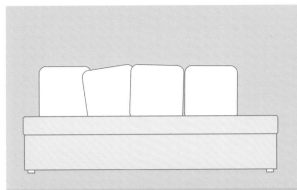

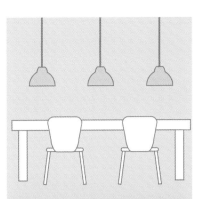

divans

A new, narrow divan can be picked up for a song in high-street bed shops and makes a great sofa, studio couch and, when required, a spare bed. Don't just throw a bedspread over it, though, or it will look like a boring bed. Instead, layer the divan with throws and load it with cushions. Alternatively, make a smart tailored cover or a fun frilly one.

Put two divans together to make a swish-looking, corner seating system, normally an expensive item. If you want your divan to function well as a sofa, invest in some good-quality back cushions.

multiple pendant lampshades

Some of these lampshades are so inexpensive that you can buy three of them for less than the price of a single more expensive version. Why not hang three or more in rows above a dining table. Alternatively, hang a single lampshade low over a table in a sparely furnished room.

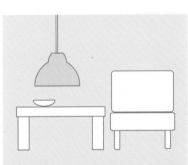

box cushions

Large, soft floor cushions are great for lolling around on, but they clutter up the space and are not much use for anything else. The newer box cushions are neater, smarter and more versatile. Some are made of firm foam and look good in plain covers whilst others are stuffed with feathers or constructed like mattresses and are often piped round the edges. These are more expensive, but three of them will probably still cost a lot less than a good quality stool, chair or bed.

Pile up a stack of three cushions to make a footstool for weary feet or an extra seat.

A purpose-designed tray top is often sold alongside the cushions. Stack your cushions and add the tray top to transform them into an occasional table.

Spread them on the floor and you have a comfortable, instant guest bed.

pendant lampshades

With an opaque metal shade, light escapes only at the base, throwing a pool of directional light. Stainless steel is cool and modern, but white and coloured enamel can be perfect in a retro or more casual environment. Translucent glass throws light out of the sides as well as the base, providing more less-directional light. Plain white-etched glass suits any style and won't detract from the room.

buying new shelving

Open shelves are an easy and efficient way of storing and displaying anything from books and saucepans to computers and clothes. Wall-mounted shelving systems are inexpensive and very versatile, but for those who can't or won't drill into walls, there are plenty of freestanding versions. Choose from wood, laminate, metal and glass to create any number of looks from rustic to sleek. Shelves will only look good if the contents are neatly or well displayed. Piles of junk just won't do, so be disciplined and use your creative instincts to create a good impression.

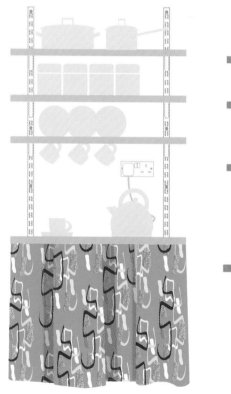

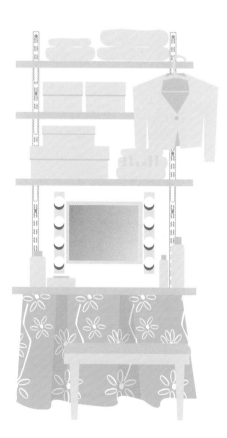

shelf ideas

wall-mounted

The simple metal upright and bracket shelving systems illustrated are readily available and inexpensive. They are easy to put up, robust, versatile and suitable for a variety of uses and locations, from hidden-away storage to open display.

Available in white, black or silver metal finish, the uprights normally come in three heights with a range of bracket sizes for different widths of shelves. They can be configured to any size and can easily be made to fit exactly into alcoves and recesses. The height of the shelves can be adjusted to accommodate both short and tall objects. A small range of fittings are available, including dividers and end sections to prevent books or objects toppling over or falling off the sides.

The largest brackets available will support a shelf deep enough to use as a worktop. Kitchen worktops, either wooden or laminate, work well but are heavy so you should therefore add extra support using screw-on legs. Packets or cans of food, utensils and crockery can look attractive, especially when displayed in storage jars, neat rows or hanging from hooks screwed to the underside of the shelves. Not everything looks good on show, so stow any unsightly things away behind a curtain hung from the worktop: this is a good way of disguising washing machines and dishwashers.

This type of shelving is also perfect for an instant, practical workstation, which can be on its own or part of a run of shelves in a kitchen, bedroom, living room or even hallway.

For a bedroom, fashion shelves into a dressing table with extra storage. Stow away clothes and accessories in good-looking boxes, which keep everything clean and dust free. Pretty it up with paint, a gathered curtain and an upholstered stool.

freestanding

Before fixing any shelves, make sure your walls can take the weight. Books in particular are very heavy, so make sure any fixing can stand the strain. If your walls aren't up to it, or if you can't or aren't allowed to drill into them, there are plenty of freestanding shelving systems and bookcases in a wide range of materials, dimensions and configurations.

Some of the cheapest systems consist of wooden uprights with the shelves suspended between. They can look a bit utilitarian but are easily smartened up with paint or stain. If you like the industrial look, opt for galvanised versions usually meant for garages and utility rooms.

Freestanding bookshelves in laminate are very inexpensive and, providing you use them confidently, preferably in rows of two or more, they look fine once they are filled up. Solid wood bookcases can be stained, painted or polished and if you want to hide things away for aesthetic or practical purposes you could rig up a roller blind or, for a cosy cottage look, a floral print curtain.

laminated board

The least expensive shelving option, consisting of chipboard with a laminated coating, usually in white, and available in a variety of widths. For a smarter, more sophisticated look, fix a piece of wood battening across the front of the shelves using panel pins, then paint or stain to fit in with the rest of your decor.

chunky wood

For a more substantial look, buy thick planks from a builders' merchant or DIY store. Sand down to a smooth finish and paint or stain.

driftwood

There is no law that says shelves have to match, so use a collection of reclaimed planks, driftwood or lucky skip finds to create something completely unique.

ready-made shelves

Some retailers sell shelving system components separately. So save money on expensive uprights by buying just the ready-made shelves in a style, material and finish that would otherwise be unavailable or difficult to achieve.

small cupboards

Incorporate small wall cupboards into a shelving system to provide concealed storage for less attractive things or, if you choose glass doors, an opportunity to display something precious.

buying new cheapskate choice

Thrift furniture can sometimes require a little alternative thinking. A separate worksurface placed on top of filing cabinets provides not only a desk with plenty of useful storage, but an opportunity to choose materials tailored to your requirements and available space. Mass-market stores and office suppliers have affordable filing cabinets, but you could also use second-hand ones, painted if necessary. Surfaces can vary from a wooden tabletop or door to a laminated worktop. Scour DIY stores for other items, such as garden furniture, which can be adapted for indoor use.

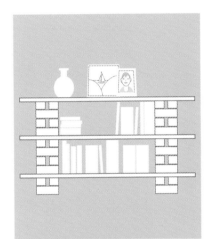

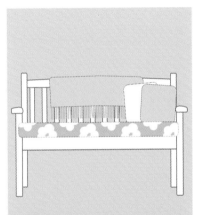

planks on bricks

A good thrift idea and perfect for the 'industrial' look, especially if you use scaffolding planks. Once a cliche, this simple construction is back in fashion. It doesn't need to be fixed to the wall, but stability is crucial so make sure you use enough bricks to form a stable construction. Bricks are heavy so if you are worried about the floor, just build a low unit.

picnic bench

Extremely good value for very little money and available at most DIY and high-street stores, as well as garden centres. Paint in thick gloss paint and use as seating in a kitchen-diner. For extra comfort, put cushions on the bench seats. These benches are quite wide so may not be suitable for very cramped spaces.

garden bench

Plain wooden garden benches can be turned into indoor seating with a coat of paint and some seat cushions. As well as looking good, extra cushions or draped throws and quilts provide added comfort. Perfect for a summery, seasidey feel and great in kitchens.

10 picture ideas

clip joint

Clip frames can look cheap, so glam them up by framing the picture within a large border using special paper. Try hand-made, textured papers or very beautiful art paper.

old prints

Look in second-hand bookshops and specialist art booksellers for old exhibition catalogues, which are usually very cheap and supply good-quality reproductions for framing.

plain and simple

Simple, aluminium or black frames look very discreet and are perfect for black-and-white photographs or drawings.

keep it simple

Sticking to a single style of frame will unify a mix of prints, paintings and photographs.

single line

A single row of pictures set halfway up the wall looks sophisticated. You don't have to keep to one size, but hang the pictures with all tops or all bottoms toeing the line.

sight lines

When hanging pictures, don't hang them too high or you won't be able to appreciate them properly. Work out the best position to view a picture from a seated as well as a standing position.

off the wall

Propping pictures against the wall gives you a different vantage point and saves making holes in the wall. Useful for covering plugs, cables and other unsightly floor-level holes or stains.

well planned

A satisfying arrangement of pictures takes time and considerable trial and error. Use the drawing programme on your PC to plot the positions of pictures on a scale drawing and save your wall from unnecessary holes.

keep control

Don't dot pictures around the place. Lining them up in disciplined rows or containing them to just one wall will give them greater impact.

shelf life

A narrow shelf is a great way to display pictures. Now widely available in wood or metal, they avoid the need for hanging; just prop up the pictures and change them around whenever you fancy.

lighting

When it comes to lighting, limited resources do not mean limited options as the range available is huge, and much of it remarkably inexpensive. The problem may be that, faced with an abundance of styles, colours and finishes, it is easy to get carried away. You are more likely to throw good light on your surroundings if you curb your enthusiasm and adopt a disciplined approach. For best results, especially in a small or open-plan home, keep to one or two styles. But you don't have to be well behaved all the time, so add some pzazz with a chandelier or coloured light show.

general illumination

Spotlights and downlighters give overall illumination. Styles vary from standard spotlights, available singly or in rows or groups of three or more, to adventurous, curved metal shapes. Recessed downlighters are popular for living areas and kitchens, look modern and give an overall wash of light, but not all ceilings are suited to these. The system, which usually operates at a different voltage and requires a separate circuit, should be installed by a professional. A good system is expensive, but can be worth the investment.

The interest in retro furnishings has led to a reappraisal of the single, central ceiling light with drum shades, glass shaded light fittings and chandeliers back in favour. If your central light is used only occasionally, it will look fine with a plain frosted glass, fabric or paper shade.

pendant lights

A longer flex on a ceiling light makes it a pendant. To save the expense of moving a light fitting, use a long flex looped through a hook screwed into the ceiling and hang the light wherever you want it. A paper lantern hung low in a corner looks good. Rows of pendant lights look trendy and are a good alternative to spotlights or downlighters in a kitchen.

wall lights

Much subtler than overhead lighting. Some require wiring into the wall, which could be an expensive bother, but there are plug-in versions too. Single plug-in, spotlights fixed in a row halfway up the wall are cheap, easy to do and can be angled to create a variety of effects.

task lighting

Desk lamps provide good illumination for reading, knitting and even cooking, but can also be angled to give general light. Floor lamps can be placed next to a chair or desk, doubling as spotlights. Keep an eye out for older versions and for new aluminium photographers' lamps, which are both cheap and stylish.

lamp bases and standard lamps

With the wide range of shades available, it is possible to create any style from antique and retro to minimal and modern. Slim metal lamp bases complement most interior styles, but ceramic lamp bases are back in fashion in all guises from fancy urns to matt, plain-coloured glazes. Old, turned, wooden lamp bases often turn up in junk shops; they can be stripped and polished or painted to be used with either a modern, plain drum shade or a pretty, patterned shade for a nostalgic effect. Make your own lamps using a lamp fitting available from DIY stores and electrical retailers. Be daringly kitsch and use a Chianti bottle or terribly arty and use a glass bowl filled with pebbles or marbles.

display lighting

Plug-in downlighters with their own transformers can be fixed underneath shelves and inside cupboards to highlight your possessions. Picture lights were once considered naff, but if you have a stunning image, why not make the most of it?

feature lights

Christmas lights, or versions of them, are easy to plug in and provide limitless possibilities. String them along shelves, behind beds, or hang across walls.

stow away

chests, boxes and trunks

One large chest can hold a lot of stuff and be used as a seat, table or surface for display. Ideal for linens and clothes, but keep moths at bay with lavender or old-fashioned moth balls. Also great for stowing unsightly equipment and tools. Give beautiful examples pride of place; disguise the more prosaic with a coat of paint or a colourful throw.

bags and baskets

Many of us have a weakness for bags and can't resist buying more. Use them for storage, hang them up shaker-style on hooks or arrange them decoratively on shelves, floors or tops of cupboards. Good for anything, including laundry, scarves, gloves, socks and shoes, knickers and tights, towels and toys.

suitcases and hampers

Old cases aren't great for taking on holiday but they are perfect for storing anything from clothes to photographs. While old ones have charm, new cases can be very chic. Decant their contents into bin liners when you need them for trips away.

storage

Whether you want to keep things safe, clean, out of sight or just like to know where everything is, storage is an important issue for every interior. Lots of storage ideas are discussed throughout this book, but there is always room for another idea and an alternative approach, so here are a few more.

clear out

Storage can be a big problem, but it is also big business. There is no shortage of storage 'solutions' available that promise to bring stylish order to our lives. But before you give in to temptation and buy a huge quantity of beautiful boxes or baskets, think carefully. Some so-called storage solutions often take up a lot of room and can become a storage problem in themselves, as well as encouraging us to keep things that would be better thrown away.

De-cluttering is not only fashionable but a good way of reducing storage needs by weeding out the unloved, unattractive and unnecessary, leaving only what you want and need.

built-in

Not everyone can afford (or wants) wall-to-wall, built-in storage or, indeed, has room for it, but it does keep things looking calm and under control even if inside the cupboards there is complete chaos. There are plenty of cheap kitchen and wardrobe units that, as long as you stick with plain designs and neutral colours, can look good – but only if they

are installed properly. Bad workmanship will emphasise cheap and weak points, so do a good job or think again and go for something more solid such as a large, freestanding cupboard or shelves fronted by a curtain or blind.

If you like the clean, clutter-free look, have particular storage needs and are planning on staying in your home for a long time, it is worth saving up for decent, bespoke or good-quality, built-in storage. Shelves are cheaper than cupboards, but not everyone wants to see what is on them. In a bedroom the alcoves or a whole wall of shelving and hanging space could be covered using roller or bamboo blinds or a curtain.

wardrobes

Minimise the wardrobe space required by storing seasonal clothes elsewhere. This not only frees up rail and shelf space, which allows clothes to hang properly and not get squashed; it also means that the stored items are kept dust free and safe from damage. Go for quantity rather than quality and buy a smaller, and therefore less expensive, wardrobe. The seasonal clothes can be kept in drawers

or attractive boxes on top of the wardrobe or under the bed.

big cupboards

A large, generous cupboard can hold a huge amount of stuff and if it is fitted out with shelves you will be able to see where everything is and be able to access it quickly and easily. Look out for old school or office examples and investigate commercial suppliers and local carpenters for new ones.

keep out

If something is beautiful or even just pleasing to the eye, display it. In a kitchen it is far easier to pick a mug off a hook or a plate off a plate rack or dresser than delve into the cupboard, and books and magazines are more likely to be read if they are kept on open shelves or are piled on a table or the floor.

make do and amend

If you have taken stock of what you've got and decided to make the most of your home and its contents, now is the time to make good the basic structure. Set in motion a programme of repairs and refinements that will provide a solid foundation for any finishing interior flourishes and show off your treasures in the best possible way.

building basics

A comprehensive tour of your home will help to assess where your priorities lie. Your tight budget may be used up with mundane repairs, but it will be a worthwhile investment. All properties respond to a little TLC – a programme of hole filling, surface smoothing and generally 'making good' followed by a coat of paint has been known to produce silk purses from sows' ears and will generate the feel-good factor.

Planning laws, building regulations and health and safety matters apply to even minor building works. Any violations of rules or mistakes in calculations are potentially dangerous, against the law and very expensive. Before embarking on any work, it is advisable, and often essential, to employ an expert in the form of an architect or structural engineer. Choose carefully – contact the relevant organisations, including your local authority, for recommended contractors – and ask to check their credentials. Building work can be the stuff of nightmares, but the pain will be lessened if you use a reputable builder, know exactly what the work entails, what to expect and have a basic knowledge of how it is to be done. This is where an expert comes in handy – some even offer to supervise the work for a fee. Though expensive, this fee could save you money and time lost through mistakes, misunderstandings and mishaps.

cost analysis

Those on a tight budget often dismiss thoughts of structural or refurbishment work, fearing that the costs are way above their means. However, small-scale works with a large impact can cost hundreds rather than thousands.

expensive
Major building works need the services of an architect, surveyor, structural engineer and good builders, as well as the approval of the local authority.

Electrics and plumbing are best done by professionals, as they involve pulling up floors and knocking holes in walls.

not as expensive as you think
Plastering and skimming should definitely be done by an expert. Although it makes a mess, it doesn't take long. Smooth walls and ceilings make a huge difference to the quality of a decorative scheme.

New floors may cause considerable disruption when laid, but a professional job by a specialist can give a dramatic effect and be well worth the expense.

Small building works, such as taking down an interior wall or building a new one, are relatively easy and surprisingly inexpensive.

very reasonable
Paint can completely transform a room, and your life, for very little cost.

Fixtures and fittings are excellent value, often well designed and come in huge ranges, including lighting, bathroom fittings and storage solutions.

free
All that you need is your labour and that of friends and family, enthusiasm and imagination.

schedule of works

Armed with a clipboard, go round your home and assess its condition. Note anything that needs attention, repair, removal or reappraisal. Poke into every corner – including the roof space, if possible – and under flooring and wallcoverings to examine the state of walls, ceilings, floors, windows, doors, fixtures and fittings.

structure

Is your home structurally sound? If necessary, hire someone to check for dry and wet rot and woodworm. Tell-tale signs are rotten wood, damp patches, mould and funny smells. It is not always obvious, so have a good poke around and, if you have access to the roof space, check joists, roof timbers and look for evidence of leaks.

floors

Take up any flooring to inspect the floors, noting all damage, damp and suitability for treatment. You never know, you may find wonderful wood, beautiful tiles or trendy lino gasping for air. Are the floorboards good enough to strip or are they better covered up? Can old wood-block floors be revived? With solid floors, is the sub-floor OK? Can tiles be repaired/replaced? Can holes be filled or is something more drastic required?

walls and ceilings

Tap surfaces to check for holes and hidden damage. Is the surface in good condition? If not, can it be put right with filler or does it need replastering? Does wallpaper need removing or can it be painted or papered over?

woodwork

Check door frames, picture rails, architraves and skirtings. Do they need rubbing down or stripping? If they are in poor condition, will a coat of paint suffice? Can they be repaired or would it be easier to replace them?

fixtures and fittings

Strip out any fittings, including built-in cupboards and shelves that are badly made, too far gone to repair or just ugly.

windows

Do they fit? Are they in good condition? Do they need replacing or just minor repairs, plus a good rub down, a coat of paint and new fittings? Are they secure? Time to put in patio doors and French windows?

doors

Do they fit and open and close properly? Do they need replacing? Do they need to be there? Would they be better hung the other way round? Would glass bring in more light? How are you going to treat them – strip, rub down, paint?

electrics

Is it safe? Do you have the latest fuse box? Do you know your circuits? Do you want to put in track lighting (in which case you will need a new circuit) or new wiring for sound or communication systems. Do you want to reroute wiring and cables so that they are safer and/or out of sight?

plumbing

Locate the stop-tap and make sure you know where the pipes are. Do you want to relocate the supply or drainage?

gas

Never touch anything to do with gas yourself. Get gas appliances checked regularly by a registered expert. Do any heaters or the boiler need updating?

heating systems

Inspect the current systems for faults or leaks. Do you want to add or move radiators or install a new type of heating.

energy eco-check

Insulation saves energy. Is your system efficient? Are there eco-alternatives?

health and safety

Do you have a smoke alarm? If not, get one now. They are cheap and easy to install. Do you have proper ventilation for gas appliances? An expert will check.

structural sense

Just as an expensive outfit is spoiled by scruffy shoes, a tatty room detracts from even the most beautiful furniture. In the priority stakes, you might be better to opt for a beautiful floor and fewer furnishings.

floors

If you want the stripped bare look, make sure the surface is sealed to minimise wear and keep out dirt and stains (see page opposite). If you have live woodworm or other suspected pests, seek advice and treat as necessary.

Stone and tiled floors respond well to a good clean: hire an industrial machine for such a tough job, then seal with a proprietary sealant or wax polish. A few small defects in a stone floor adds to its character, but missing tiles are not so charming. If available, fill in any gaps with replacement tiles. If not, use heavy-duty filler or concrete mix.

Bare concrete can be a much smarter alternative to tatty carpet or vile vinyl, but it must be sealed to keep in potentially harmful dust. Give the floor a good scrub, fill in any cracks and holes, then coat with a clear sealant or floor paint.

Good-quality carpet is worth keeping and, if it is not too threadbare or stained, industrial cleaning works wonders. If you are taking up your carpet, avoid too much waste by cutting up any good bits and making them into rugs. The edges need to be cut very neatly, but would look better still trimmed with carpet or binding tape.

Old linoleum and vinyl complement the fashionable retro look. They can be given a new lease of life with a good scrub and a coating of sealant or polish.

walls

If you think your bare plaster can pass muster as 'delightfully distressed' then leave your walls alone. Otherwise, even out any holes with an all-purpose filler then replaster or skim, if necessary. Don't worry too much about uneven surfaces, small defects won't show under a couple of coats of paint or wallpaper.

woodwork

Damaged window frames, architraves and skirting boards can spoil an otherwise attractive interior. Smaller defects can be repaired using wood filler but more severe damage may require a patch using a matching moulding.

New architraves and skirting pull a room together and do not cost very much. For a crisp, clean look use square-edged lengths of wood – deep and chunky, if you like.

windows

The style and state of the windows have a huge effect on an interior scheme. Original windows obviously look best as they were designed to complement the architectural style and proportions of the building. Poor quality or inappropriate replacement windows can seriously affect the value of your house. Sensible and sensitive owners are taking them out and reverting to architecturally correct, period style or good-quality new equivalents. If you don't own your house or flat, or changing windows is just too expensive, opt for a disguise using shutters, blinds, metal mesh, wooden or fabric screens and panels.

doors

New doors are not expensive but don't go for the ready finished variety, they look cheap and nasty. Traditional panelled designs suit older properties but flat, flush finishes give a more modern look. If the doors are an important architectural feature of your house and have been removed or defaced, save up for the real thing from salvage yards or specialist dealers. In the 1950s and early '60s it was fashionable to cover panelled doors with hardboard so check to see what, if anything, is behind a plain facade.

5 frugal floors

stripped

One of the easiest ways to smarten a room is to strip existing floorboards and seal them with paint, varnish, wax or oil. If the boards are in good shape and a pleasing colour, a matt varnish will give a warm yet clean look. For a dramatic statement, use a dark or coloured stain – exercise caution, however, as it can be oppressive. Floor paint is now available in a wide range of colours. Although some ranges are pricey, they do give a dense, smooth finish that will cover most imperfections.

chipboard

This material is used in newly built homes as a base intended to be covered with carpet, laminates or tiles but can look great used on its own and sealed with varnish or paint. A cheaper alternative to new floorboards, it comes in large sections with a tongue-and-groove joint for efficient joining and a neat appearance. It can be laid directly onto joists or battens on top of concrete. Take the opportunity to put polystyrene underneath for extra insulation of heat and sound.

laminated

This easy-to-lay flooring is very popular and has helped provide homes across the land with the 'light and airy' feel. Some are extremely cheap but be careful as the surface is rarely real wood, instead it is a photograph printed on to laminate which, while convincing, will wear off in areas of high traffic in a relatively short time. Also, floors need to breathe, and many people have discovered that underneath a 'well-fitted' laminate floor condensation has rotted the joists.

tiles

The advantage of tiles is that they are extremely hard-wearing and therefore a thrifty option. Also, the development of thinner tiles makes them easier to cut and lay, and flexible grouting means that a concrete sub-floor is no longer essential. There is a huge variety available including stone and slate, traditional quarry tiles and plain or decorated ceramic.

carpet

Fitted carpet is often the cheapest and most sensible option; fortunately it is back in fashion. Not only does it cover a multitude of sins, it is also warm and absorbs sound. Go for 100% wool, rather than synthetic, and stick to plain, neutral colours. Sea-grass and other natural fibres are usually more expensive and need to be stuck down, adding to the expense; also they hold dirt and can't be cleaned as easily as wool.

prudent decorator

Providing you don't go in for too many specialist paints or particularly swanky wallpaper, decorating need not be an expensive business. Prudent painters use colour and a clean background as a basis for thrifty good looks.

preparation

The toughest and most tedious part of decorating is the preparation. The time and effort invested in preparing surfaces and woodwork are rewarded with a finish that not only looks better but last longer.

Walls and ceilings that are in good condition only require a quick dust down. If they are very dirty, or covered in remnants of wallpaper, they should be washed down with a warm, mild solution of detergent, followed by plain water. Woodwork should be rubbed down using abrasive paper or washed with sugar soap to break down the hard surface and provide a 'key' for the new coat of paint.

You can save money and effort by leaving any woodwork unpainted. Some evidence of age, including chips and flakes, can be attractive, but dirty and tacky paintwork is not. Wash woodwork down to remove any fingermarks and goo.

Untreated wood and metal need to be given a coat of primer before painting. This protects the material and provides a good base for paint. The available range of primers has expanded to include those suitable for shiny surfaces, such as melamine. These are perfect for the thrifty as they enable you to paint over kitchen cupboards, tiles and any items finished with a hard, shiny varnish.

paint points

Buy your paints from one of the large manufacturers – they are often cheaper and the colours are helpfully grouped to make selection easier. Normally, emulsion paint is used on walls, with gloss or eggshell on woodwork. Modern emulsion paints, especially the washable varieties, can also be used on woodwork that is not exposed to high wear.

Available in a matt or silk finish, emulsion is water-based and therefore easy to apply. Gloss paint dries to a hard shiny finish, it is more viscous and consequently trickier to use. Gloss is very hard-wearing and lasts a long time, so unless you want to change the colour, it won't always have to be redone every time you redecorate. Eggshell or satin finish paint has a softer, matter finish and is easier to apply than gloss, but is not so hard-wearing. Traditionally, gloss and eggshell paints have been spirit-based, making them smelly and a potential health hazard. These paints are now being phased out, and water-based, low VOCs versions introduced, which are more pleasant to use and dry much quicker.

posh paint

There is no doubt that some specialist paint ranges include the most wonderful colours and give a distinctly different finish. If paint is your passion, it may well be worth the extra expense. Architecturally beautiful houses should always be treated with respect and, as well as being historically correct, some of these paints will enhance a building's appearance.

wallpaper

The good news is that wallpaper – perfect for covering poor, uneven surfaces – is back in fashion. The bad news is that the best papers are very expensive. Thrifty options include papering just one wall, finding a lucky bargain in a sale or using a cheaper paper. This third option is tricky as it is difficult to find a good cheap papers. The once-despised palm fronds and spriggy flowers came back into fashion just as they were being banished from the ranges of the mass-market producers and retailers. They have returned, but unfortunately they have been repackaged as trendy with a higher price tag.

stencil

A cheaper way to cover a wall with pattern is stencilling. Avoid anything twee or complicated. Exercise subtlety with simple designs and tones of one colour or a family of colours rather than a whole paintbox.

get creative

Plain walls are all very well but occasionally you may fancy something a bit different, so don't hold back. Indulge your creative urges and get arty or, for the more pragmatic, use the wall as extra storage or display.

cuttings edge

Turn one wall into a giant scrapbook – the perfect place for all those cuttings you've never got round to putting in a proper book. Do the same with your favourite photographs and postcards. Depending on the state of the wall, stick them up with tacks or wall-tack, but try to maintain some sort of order and method to stop it looking a mess.

mapped out

Maps are large, colourful and fairly cheap. They are also informative and offer the opportunity to brush up on your geography, plan a trip or study a place you know and love. World maps tend to be brightly coloured with lots of blue sea, but for a more sophisticated effect choose the subtle green tones of an ordinance survey map.

museum piece

Don't hide your treasures away. Whether they are china dogs, stamps, model airplanes or driftwood, get out your cherished collections and put them where you can admire them. An edited selection will look chic but why not go that little bit further and cover an entire wall with a display using shelves or glass-fronted cupboards. They don't need to match.

hang it all

Wall hangings are great decoration and conveniently cover up poor or unattractive surfaces. They can add character to a plain room as well as a bit of extra warmth. What you hang on your wall depends on what you've got – it could be a rug, dhurry, kelim, embroidered panel, piece of appliqué, patchwork or just a piece of nice fabric. It can be home-made or something picked up in a souk, ethnic shop or furniture superstore.

hang-ups

Do the shaker thing and fix a row of pegs around your walls to hang your chairs upon. This keeps the floor clear for that uncluttered look. The chairs will of course stick out into the room, so if space is very limited, use folding chairs. Add a folding table and you could hang up a whole dining suite.

kitchens culinary choice

The thrift philosophy involves prioritising, so the amount you spend on your kitchen should be determined by how much time you spend in it and how it fits in to your lifestyle. Installing a brand new kitchen is a major expense, so think hard before making any decisions. Freshly painted walls, new ceramic tiles and a revived floor – which would be included in most new schemes anyway – might just be enough to give the existing kitchen units a new lease of life.

top priority

If the kitchen really is the heart of your home, be prepared to lavish the majority of your budget on this one room. Spend wisely, taking time and advice on the best way to do so.

If you do a lot of cooking, put an oven, work surfaces and storage at the top of your priority list. If you do tear out your old kitchen, avoid replacing it with a cheap and cheerful option as generally they aren't terribly robust – edges, trims and hinges will soon show signs of wear. Go for units in solid wood or high-quality laminates with good carcasses, hinges, runners, doors and drawer fittings.

A designer fridge-freezer may seem extravagant if it only holds ready meals and Champagne, but if it is crammed with the ingredients for top-quality meals then you will be getting your money's worth. New range-style cookers are great for serious cooks but don't be fooled by the cheaper versions; invest in whichever is better if not the best.

fast food

If you are a busy person with no interest in cooking, who seldom entertains at home and only uses the kitchen for hot drinks and serving up takeaways, inexpensive units will suffice as they won't be subjected to intense wear and tear. Go for a small, galley-style kitchen or a minimal kitchen housed along one wall to free up space for other purposes.

Lifestyles and circumstances do change, however, so if you think you are likely to spend more time in the kitchen in the future, make allowances and invest in something altogether more hard-wearing and hardworking.

layout

There are lots of rules on kitchen layouts involving work triangles and what or what not to put where, but rooms and lives are not always quite so standardised. The layout of a kitchen will be determined to a great extent on the space available, the position of any plumbing, windows and doors. Kitchen suppliers will plan your room for you, but don't assume they know best – their job is to sell units and they often over-prescribe in the storage department. If your want your kitchen to be a sociable area, it may be better to have fewer units in favour of a large table, which serves as work surface and storage, as well as entertaining or work space.

materials

Advanced production techniques and an expanding market have made materials that were once deemed luxury, and therefore expensive, widely available at realistic prices. Materials such as limestone, slate and terrazzo are now available in thinner tiles suitable for walls, worktops and floors. Convincing imitations of these luxury materials in the form of ceramic tiles and laminates are now also widespread.

Likewise, new manufacturing processes have also placed solid wooden worktops within range of smaller budgets. Providing you treat them regularly with oil, they will last for years. The disadvantage of laminated units has always been the edges, where poor joins and a tendency to chip eventually show up their shortcomings. New techniques for spray-coating fibreboards now give a better, longer-lasting finish. Etched glass looks sophisticated and modern and is being used very successfully even at the cheaper end of the market.

5 thrifty tips

A new layout doesn't necessarily mean throwing everything out and starting again. Faced with a kitchen full of units that aren't in the best state of repair, why not redesign the space using only the good stuff and then smarten it all up with new worktop.

An extra-thick, good-quality worktop may cost more but can make ordinary units look expensive. Likewise, it can pull a motley collection of fittings into some sort of order.

Fix a long metal pole to the wall or spanning the width of a narrow kitchen or alcove. Then buy a batch of butchers' hooks and hang up all your pots, pans, utensils and sundry items.

Hooks are cheap and a row of them is ideal for tea towels, aprons, shopping bags, coats, dog leads and other paraphernalia. Hanging bags and baskets also provide extra space for storage.

If you can't afford or don't want base units, a curtain will hide appliances and open shelves. Gathered gingham or a flowery print will look either nostalgic or downright pretty, while plain or striped linen or cotton, ungathered, with eyelets and threaded on to a metal pole will look minimal and modern.

kitchens door handles

It's a relatively easy decision to replace a kitchen that is in bad repair and doesn't meet your needs for storage and layout, but what do you do if the existing fittings are in fine fettle, but just look tired and dated? Ripping out a perfectly good kitchen is wasteful as well as ecologically unsound, but it is possible to revive and restore doors and drawer fronts with paint or stain and by adding new handles and knobs.

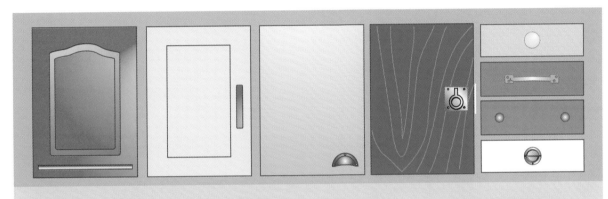

doors and drawers

There are a number of new primers available, which ensure that paint will stick to shiny, non-porous surfaces. This means you can even paint over laminates. A facelift will only work well if you take care to do a good paint job. Before painting, take off all hinges and handles and don't forget to do both sides.

You can update old solid wooden units with a dramatic dark stain, but you will have to sand off any varnish and take great care not to get a patchy look.

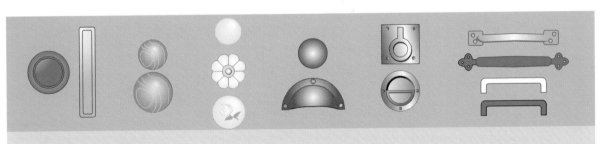

knobs and handles

Choose from a huge range from the large DIY and furniture chains, as well as more specialist shops. Removing old handles will leave holes in the doors and drawers, so your choice of replacement and where you position them may be restricted.

As well as modern, minimal – which will add class to any dull unit – look out for retro plastic or chunky rustic handles. Dare to be different with decorated porcelain or antique knobs. Simple metal pull handles and locker fittings will look shipshape.

kitchens alternative remedies

While fitted kitchens are neat and efficient, they can lack character, and sometimes they just don't suit your taste, lifestyle, house or the space available. In addition, drilling into walls may not be an option if the walls are uneven, not strong enough or too nice to cover up. As well as the wider availability of free-standing, unfitted kitchen furniture, there is the opportunity to make up your own idiosyncratic style using a mixture of furniture, fittings and finds garnered from bargain-hunting forays, new pieces and inherited favourites. Take a new look at what is on offer and use a bit of ingenuity and flair, plus perhaps a coat of paint to put together something a little bit different which needn't cost the earth.

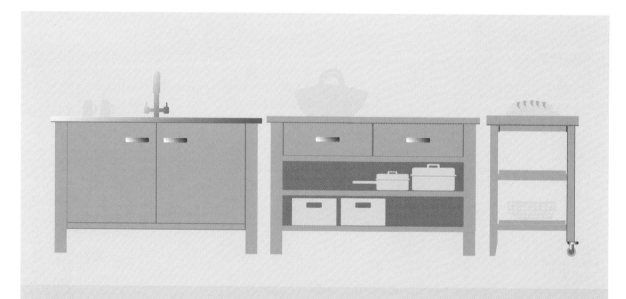

unfitted

The great economical advantage of an unfitted kitchen is that you can take it with you when you move home. What's more, you don't have to drill any holes into your walls, or even have good walls, and you can move the furniture around to suit any changing circumstances or on a whim.

An added bonus is that an unfitted kitchen can be added to over a period of time, as and when you can afford it.

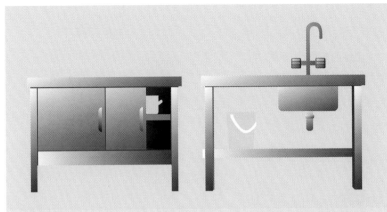

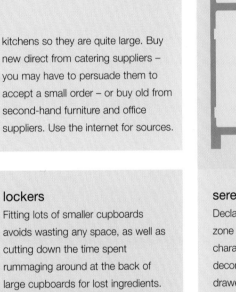

catering

Stainless-steel, high-quality catering units cost a fraction of the price of the posher domestic versions. They are normally of a very practical and unfussy design, but bear in mind they are for use in restaurant and school kitchens so they are quite large. Buy new direct from catering suppliers – you may have to persuade them to accept a small order – or buy old from second-hand furniture and office suppliers. Use the internet for sources.

lockers

Fitting lots of smaller cupboards avoids wasting any space, as well as cutting down the time spent rummaging around at the back of large cupboards for lost ingredients. Lockers make an unusual and efficient alternative to standard kitchen units. They tend to be narrower than standard cupboards, so they make good use of small spaces. Available in metal or wood, buy new from specialist suppliers, where you will be able to choose from a range of colours, or keep a lookout for old office and school equipment.

serendipity

Declaring your kitchen a unit-free zone makes for a more personal, characterful and possibly cheaper decorating scheme. Chests of drawers, large cupboards and dressers are all great for storage. One large cupboard can house everything including pots, pans, china, equipment and food. A redundant chest of drawers is great for storing a wide variety of stuff, from notebooks and crayons to 'unruly' ingredients, such as packets of rice, pulses and pasta.

kitchens plus

Changing lifestyles and the high premium on space have led to changes in how rooms are allocated and used. A tendency towards fewer, bigger rooms, rather than several small ones, has meant less activity-specific areas and more multi-functional rooms. Kitchens are no longer just places for cooking or washing, but are used for work and socialising too. It can be a tight squeeze, but many are opting to create an open-plan combination kitchen area.

+ dine

In a small kitchen, a fold-down table and a couple of stools hung on the wall will free up space for cooking but allow you to eat in comfort. A breakfast bar is easier to fit in and can be fixed at normal table or bar height. If there is no room for a farmhouse-scale table, opt for something long and narrow and use benches instead of chairs.

+ live

Kitchens can be cosy, sociable places and the perfect place for a sofa, armchairs, the TV and sound system. If space is a problem, it may be possible to squeeze in just one armchair (why not make it a rocking chair?), or build in a bench or window seat. Failing that, make dining chairs comfortable enough for prolonged stays.

+ work

A kitchen can be a good place for a bit of peace and quiet and the ideal environment in which to work. Whether its doing homework, paying the bills or even your way of earning a living, a kitchen workspace can be a table that doubles as a desk, a designated section of worktop with space underneath for a stool, or a whole mini-office in a cupboard to protect computers and equipment from steam. Even a fold-down table will provide enough space for a laptop computer.

+ play

Even if you have a large sitting room, the chances are that children will end up around your feet when you are in the kitchen. If you are knocking two rooms together, think about opening up or adding space next to the kitchen to create a play area where you can keep an eye on them while getting on with the chores. For small children, a way of penning them in with a gate or low partition will keep them safe from the potential dangers of cooking and appliances.

+ active

For a kitchen that turns into a studio for painting, pottery or other artistic pursuits, keep surfaces clear and easy to clean. A double sink minimises the risk of unsuitable or dangerous ingredients entering the food chain. A large expanse of kitchen floor can be just the place for yoga or exercises, and for less active pursuits, a large kitchen table is an ideal meeting place for book club or committee meetings.

bathrooms freshen-ups

Design expectations in the bathroom area are much higher now than they used to be. Bringing a tired and not-very-hygienic-looking bathroom up to scratch doesn't have to be too expensive, providing your aim is for something pleasant and functional rather than hip and flashy.

coat of paint

If your bathroom floor, walls and fittings are in generally good condition, a coat of paint could be all that's needed to make it look better, or even sensational. The bathroom is the one place eminently suited to the white-box treatment; a liberal application of brilliant white paint, which could also include the floor, will make the space look and feel fresh and hyper-hygienic. Alternatively, a small bathroom offers the opportunity to go mad and use intense colours.

accessorise

An obvious thrifty way to smarten up a lacklustre but perfectly functional bathroom is with smart, matching accessories. Even the low-price, high-street chains and supermarkets now sell good-quality ranges of plain bathroom accessories at bargain prices. A new toilet-roll holder, towel rail, shower curtain and toothbrush holder can work wonders, as can a new toilet seat, mirror and bathroom cabinet. For a modern look, stainless-steel and white-coated steel accessories work best. A cosy or nostalgic bathroom can cope with wood,

especially if it is painted or fashionably shabby. Look out for small, pretty cupboards and shelves in markets and junk shops. Matching towels smarten up any bathroom and there is no good excuse for holding back in this department as these can be picked up at very low prices everywhere from big stores, supermarkets, high-street chains and market stalls.

irony

If you are stuck with hideous wall tiles or a coloured bathroom suite that refuses to look trendy, then go for excess. Make a virtue out of disadvantage and celebrate those pink tiles with extra-fluffy pink towels, bath mat and outrageous wallpaper, featuring cabbage roses or sailing ships. Don't forget to include the bath panel in the scheme of things.

small is affordable

A small space provides the chance to use luxurious materials that would be prohibitively expensive over a large area. Consider limestone, marble or slate for floors as well as walls and other surfaces. One roll of expensive but exceptionally

beautiful wallpaper will be enough for a small bathroom, and the same goes for a specialist paint in that must-have colour.

tile tips

Ceramic tiles are relatively inexpensive, providing you stick to plain ones. Putting them up is a straightforward DIY job as long as you stick to thin tiles that can be easily cut. Taking off old tiles can be a difficult and messy business, but if you don't want the bother you can add new tiles on top of the old. The grouting between tiles tends to become grubby over time, but applying new grouting is simple and cheap. If you want something different, use a contrasting colour – white with dark tiles or a soft grey with white are both effective.

light effect

A distinctly average bathroom can be transformed with lighting, but safety is a key issue wherever electricity and water is concerned. Any new fittings should be installed by an expert, which could be expensive but may still be cheaper than more drastic improvements. Good lighting is essential for make-up and shaving.

fresh start checklist

If your existing bathroom is beyond the pale, it is often easier to strip everything out and start again. Good-quality, well-designed, simple bathroom suites, comprising of a toilet, basin and bath, are surprisingly cheap as are taps and shower fittings.

floor

Take up any old floor coverings and check for damp and rot. Bare boards can be painted using gloss or floor paint. A solid wood floor is fine as long as it is sealed to prevent water damage, but wood laminates aren't good in a bathroom as they will lift when wet. Tiles are good and in a small space you can indulge in luxury limestone, slate or ceramic. Vinyl is waterproof but if you plan to DIY, cutting and laying it around the fittings can be tricky. A concrete floor can be sealed and painted with floor paint, but fill in any holes and cracks first.

walls

Before painting, papering or tiling walls, seal any damp patches using a proprietary sealant. Emulsion and gloss paints are waterproof, but any build-up of soap is not so easy to remove. Water-resistant, wipe-down wallpaper is quite thick and good for covering uneven or stained surfaces but may start to peel if ventilation is poor. Tiles are the perfect wall covering for bathrooms. As long as you stick to plain-coloured, slim tiles, the cost will not be too high. It is advisable to tile from floor to ceiling in showers, whereas splashback panels are sufficient for baths and basins. Tiling all walls to splash-back height creates a very easy-to-clean, hygienic environment.

ventilation

If you have mould, mildew or fungus, it is probably due to bad ventilation. Opening a window is sometimes enough but you may need to install a fan or vent.

plumbing

Moving pipework is costly but worth the expense if the new layout improves your home. Starting from scratch provides a good opportunity for rerouting and concealing pipework as well as installing a new bath, shower, toilet or extra basin.

shower versus bath

While some love a long soak in a bath, others prefer the convenience of a short shower. It is tempting to free up space in a small bathroom by dispensing with the bath, but think twice. There are times when a bath is best – bathing young children or soothing tired muscles, for example. When you come to sell your house, the absence of a bath could reduce its value. A shower over the bath is a good compromise, as long as you have a glass screen or generous shower curtain to contain the water. Alternatively, consider a special small bath with a seat, which combines the activities of bathing and showering.

bathroom suites

White is best and simple is better, especially if your budget is limited. Steel baths are heavier and slightly more expensive than plastic, but they are a better buy as they last longer and don't creak alarmingly when you climb in. Avoid fancy details, such as shell-shaped soap holders and ugly bath panels. Shower trays are normally sold separately and come in a range of sizes. Ceramic is easier to clean, but weight could be a problem.

fitting the bill

Super-sophisticated taps and shower fittings can cost the earth, but there are good, well-designed, modern-looking taps available at modest prices. Or you could splash out on expensive fittings, the outlay won't be huge as you will only need one toilet-roll holder, a few hooks and a towel rail. Mirrors make a bathroom feel bigger and more glamorous. Large mirror panels are available in the DIY stores, enabling you to cover a whole wall for a small sum.

furniture restore and repair

Old and not-so-old furniture benefits from a little tender loving care, being reborn as good as new or even in a different guise. Just a little damage can reduce the value of an item quite considerably, so if you have the time, skill and patience to take on a restoration project there are some good bargains to be had.

Before buying anything, assess what you may be letting yourself in for. If the item in question is very beautiful, good quality, a rarity or an antique and you are handy with tools, you may wish to tackle the job with the help of an instruction book. It may be worth enrolling on an evening or day class so you can carry out repairs under supervision. Another option is to give the job to a skilled local carpenter or upholsterer. Although not cheap, the final cost may still work out less than buying the equivalent in good or mint condition.

upholstery

A new loose cover and a few tacks may be all that's required to bring a sofa or armchair back to life. However, if any springs are sticking through the underside or there is a serious stuffing deficiency, it will be a bigger, more complex job to put right. For dining chairs this can be reasonably straightforward, but for large sofas and armchairs buy the book, take a class or get it done professionally.

loose legs and joints

As long as there isn't too much damage to the leg ends or pieces to be glued,

fixing loose joints is a simple task. Castors can be replaced – look for old ones in second-hand and junk shops. Seek advice on the best types of glue.

drawers

It isn't particularly easy to replace split or missing drawer bottoms, so think before you buy. Providing the frame is not damaged, a clean-up, some sanding down or planing and candle wax applied to the runners will improve the fit of most drawers. Handles are easy to replace and can change an item's character as well.

wood, veneers and laminates

Solid wood can be stripped, scrubbed or sanded to bring out its original colour and grain before rewaxing or oiling. While it is possible to repair damaged veneer, it is a fiddly, skilled job. Old coloured laminates are often chipped and can't be repaired, so you have to decide whether the damage is part of a piece's charm.

wash, wax and oil

There are proprietary products specially formulated for washing wood and valuable pieces that remove dirt and discoloured

wax; you would be wise to use them. If not, a warm solution of gentle detergent (eco-varieties are good) will suffice. Use a soft, long-bristled brush to get into nooks and crannies. For stubborn dirt and stains, use a scouring pad. Rinse off the soap and dry thoroughly with a cloth. Apply Danish or finishing oil or a good-quality wax polish to bare wood. If you plan to paint the wood, first apply a coat of primer. For painted surfaces, either seal the existing paint with a thin coat of wax or apply fresh paint directly on top of the clean surface.

strip

Old painted furniture can be full of charm, but beautiful wood should be liberated from suffocating coats of paint or varnish. Stripping is fiddly and messy as it involves the use of caustic chemicals, which are corrosive and give off unpleasant fumes. Be careful. Buy a good product, follow the instructions to the letter and wear protective gloves, clothing and the correct type of mask. Don't rush the job. Don't try to remove the paint before it has properly softened as it will only require more stripper to get all the paint off.

simple chair repairs

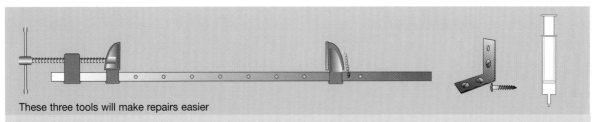

These three tools will make repairs easier

You will need a clamp to keep all parts in position while the glue dries. Small right-angled metal brackets can be used to strengthen joins and frames as an alternative to glueing or to add extra support. A syringe is great for getting glue into nooks and crannies.

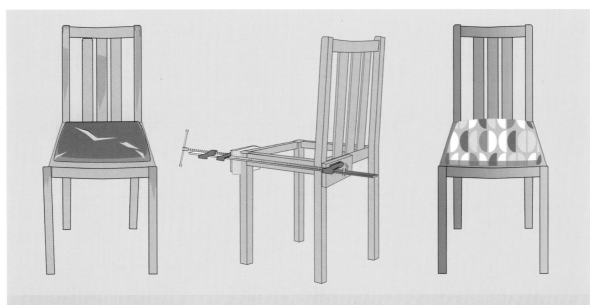

Chairs such as these are usually very cheap and plentiful and as they are well made and robust they can easily be rehabilitated. Take out the seat pad and clean down the frame, stripping off any varnish if necessary. Check all the joints and, if loose, glue them in place using a clamp. Use the clamp vertically when gluing joints on the top rail. Treat the repaired chair frame with oil or wax. Remove the existing seat cover, including as many of the old tacks as possible. Add more padding to the seat if necessary and cover with new upholstery fabric by pulling it over the frame and tacking into position underneath. Do bear in mind that if you intend to sell on any item of furniture, then all stuffing, padding and upholstery fabrics must be flame retardant.

furniture finishing touch

waxes and oils

Applying wax or oil protects wood, gives it a better, mellower colour and revives older pieces. There are a confusing number of proprietary products for treating wood – which you choose will depend on the finish you require and the state of the wood you are treating. These products are either wax- or oil-based. Waxes dry to a hard finish and can be buffed to a shiny coating that keeps out dirt and protects against scratches. Oil soaks into the wood and gives a soft, matt finish. New softwood, from which much cheap furniture is made, is normally finished with a coat of hard-wearing varnish to protect and colour the wood. This coating is not very flattering and looks cheap. Rubbing with abrasive paper will break down this surface and allow oil to penetrate, giving the wood a subtler, more natural finish.

Danish or finishing oils

A thinnish liquid that is easy to apply with a brush or cloth, oils form a water-resistant surface and prevent woods drying out and splitting. Essential for treating new wooden worktops, oils should be reapplied at regular intervals to keep wood in good condition. Oils can also be used on wooden furniture, shelves and fittings.

liquid waxes

When wax is dissolved in solvent, it is easier to apply. Most liquid waxes have a stain added – usually light, medium or dark. Liquid waxes are useful for putting life back into dry wood and toning down or deepening its colour. Some dry to a hard finish, so check on the tin.

beeswax polishes

The best furniture polish is made from beeswax, blended with solvent and perfumed with lavender or lemon. Go for the purest blend and avoid products containing silicone as this forms a surface build-up that is difficult to remove.

wood stains

Does exactly what it says on the tin. Choose from light yellow pine through to almost-black ebony. Paler tones are safer but dark stains can look sensational providing you apply them evenly, which can be tricky over large areas. Once applied, stains cannot be removed, so know what you are letting yourself in for.

age gracefully

There is a lot of reasonably priced new and second-hand repro furniture around, including tables, chairs and some quite grand-looking beds. While the shapes and quality are fine, the finish is often crude, making it look naff rather than elegant. However, with a bit of work, they can be improved and rehabilitated. Remove hard varnished or gilded surfaces using abrasive paper, steel wool and, if necessary, paint stripper. Use abrasive paper to smooth down and soften all sharp edges, including any decorative mouldings. Wash thoroughly and allow to dry before applying wax or oil for a natural finish or a coat of primer before painting with an eggshell paint – creamy white or pastels look best.

varnishes

Use clear varnish for a finish that is hard-wearing and waterproof. There are many different types to choose from but a matt finish is best. Many varnishes are polyurethane-based so will darken paint colours and add a yellowy tinge to white. To avoid this, use an acrylic varnish on a painted surface.

finishing school

These techniques can be used on all furniture, from small shelves to large cupboards. The larger the item, the better the quality of finish needs to be, so brush up your technique before tackling any large-scale projects.

gloss

The shiny look went out of favour for a while, but this hard-wearing, solid colour finish is perfect for smartening up or adding character to plain pieces. Before painting, apply a primer to bare wood and in order to achieve an even colour use an undercoat (a coat of emulsion will do). Follow with two or more coats of gloss. Rub down between each coat using fine wire wool or abrasive paper. For an even finish, use vertical brushstrokes only.

emulsion

As well as being cheaper, emulsion paint is easier to use. Though not as robust as eggshell or gloss, emulsion can be used on furniture if you seal the surface with either a clear varnish or wax polish. Beeswax polish gives a soft sheen finish which will improve and harden with regular polishing. For good colours and finishes, use specialist paints.

specialist paints

There are some wonderful specialist paints around, many of which are based on traditional recipes and made from more natural ingredients. Not only do they have a colour intensity, subtlety and a finish that is not possible with the more chemically based paints, they are also a healthier option. They are low in VOCs (volatile organic compounds). Water-based versions of eggshell and gloss are also available. Distempers and casein paints (based on the old milk paints) have a soft, chalky finish that, when used on furniture, will need to be finished with a coat of acrylic varnish (avoid polyurethane as it will darken the colour and make white look yellow). Eggshell gives a soft sheen and dead flat oil paint has a dense matt finish.

crackle glaze

Products that give a crackle effect can be bought from craft shops, specialist decorators and some DIY stores. Finishes vary from quite crude to very subtle. Application varies according to the brand, but the process involves painting the crackle glaze on top of paint, causing it to craze, and then rubbing on a darker colour paint or wax to reveal the crackle lines. Use emulsion as it goes on easier and dries quicker. For good colour effects, use small sample pots of specialist paints.

distressing

To achieve a worn look, apply a coat of paint followed by another different colour on top then, using fine wire wool, rub off some of the top coat along the edges and other areas of high wear. Alternatively, after the first coat of paint, rub the edges and patches with a wax candle to resist the second coat of paint. To give the appearance of several layers of old, chipped paint, continue the process using a different colour each time.

If you are desperate to use some of the gorgeous papers around, why not paper the inside of a cupboard or wardrobe or use them to line your drawers?

You may be lucky enough to find a collection of splendid old wallpaper samples. The back of a cupboard door is the perfect place to stick them as you can admire them without interfering with the rest of the decor.

paper pleasures

If decoupage conjures up images of rosebuds and lampshades, think again. Forget cutting out small shapes and motifs; use sheets or lengths of paper in a bolder way. There are so many wonderful designs, patterns and effects available in paper form as wallpaper, gift-wrap, hand-made and art and craft papers, it seems silly not to make the most of them. The decoupage principle remains the same: stick on the paper using wallpaper paste or spraymount and cover with a protective coating of clear varnish. If you tire of it after a while, it is not too difficult to remove.

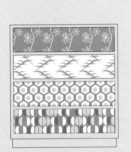

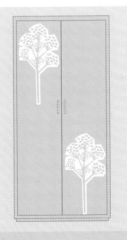

chest

Jazz up an inexpensive, plain wooden chest of drawers using different papers on each drawer front. If the paper isn't as wide as the drawers, you will have to join pieces, but don't worry too much about matching it exactly as it will add to the crazy feel. If jazz isn't your style, try art or hand-made papers.

wardrobe

There are some wonderful wallpapers around with huge motifs that can be cut out and stuck to a dull wardrobe to give it a lift. You may have a length left over from a serious wallpapering job or have found a bargain, but if not you could decide to buy a single roll. Or try asking for a sample.

door

There is no law that says doors have to be plain. If you only want a small amount of pattern in a room or you only have a limited amount of paper, the door is as good a place as any to make your statement. For an over-the-top, overall look, paper the walls as well, and watch the door disappear.

frugal fabrics

While we may be confident in choosing clothes that suit us and are comfortable, often we show less assurance when it comes to dressing our homes. Following the same fashion preferences and applying the same dress rules to your decor is likely to be more successful than getting hung up on interior fads – look inside your wardrobe and the glossy fashion magazines for inspiration.

textile style

The hardest thing about buying fabrics is what to choose. Sometimes a fabric will dictate an entire decorative scheme, but whatever its role, keep your mind on how it will fit in to the general scheme of things.

Fabrics provide the finish for an interior, giving it warmth and character. Depending on your requirements and preferences, textiles can be a barely noticeable presence or a striking main feature. Good-quality fabrics can be very expensive but there is plenty of choice in the cheaper bracket, so thrift-conscious decorators still have several options.

You could choose to use a beautiful, pricey fabric but limit it to small quantities – a short ungathered curtain, a simple blind, a single chair cover or an individual cushion. If you prefer a more opulent look, go for cheaper fabrics. Charity shops and house clearance sales sometimes have great bargains from a bygone age ready for a comeback. Alternatively, check out curtain exchanges, where you can often find elaborate curtains that can be unpicked and made into less fussy creations or used in all their glory as the star turn in a plain arena.

How you use fabric, and how much you use, depends on your chosen style. For the pared-down look, plain and simple curtains and blinds or window panels in a similar colour to the walls will blend into the background and won't spoil the clean lines.

Fabrics are an ideal means of adding decoration in the form of colour and texture – jolly up your interior with either the latest designer patterns or pretty prints and chintzes. If you want to make a statement, add a touch of drama using a stunning colour or bold print for curtains, throws or a wall hanging. A length of fabric can work wonders in detracting from unattractive surroundings, disguising ugly furnishings or hiding equipment, appliances or a nasty mess.

Your choice of fabric type will depend on its intended use. Covers for chairs, sofas and footstools need to be made in a robust fabric in order to withstand normal wear and tear, plus any extra demands such as children, pets or the accommodation of weary feet. Closely woven cottons and linens are ideal as many are washable – a useful thrifty attribute.

If you buy new upholstery, the retailer will insist that the fabric conforms to regulations related to fire risk and should have an appropriate certificate. This doesn't apply to home-made chair or sofa covers, but it might be a good idea to check the small print of your insurance policy just in case.

The notion of formal curtain fabrics has long gone out of the window – nowadays anything goes, so be imaginative. Cushions and throws provide the opportunity, and perhaps the inspiration, to do some sewing, so try your hand at patchwork, appliqué or quilting. Don't forget beds, which can look smart and fashionable or downright sexy and alluring dressed with a variety of cushions, quilts, valances, covered headboards and even curtains and canopies. Silk-lined walls may be a bit over the top but you can hang fabric in the form of a wall hanging or large panel, or you could tack it to the wall as a more permanent feature.

fabric file

natural fibres

Plain cottons and linens, including denim, are great for everything from upholstery to curtains and can normally be washed easily to keep them looking good.

textured weaves

Crunchy cotton and linen weaves allow you to add variety using texture.

wools

Wool tweed, suiting and cashmere are chic but often require specialist cleaning.

traditional prints

Chintz and toile de jouy look cosy in a traditional country cottage way, while spriggy flowers have a fresh appeal. Provençal prints are bright and cheerful and can be picked up cheaply.

luxury

Velvets, silks and damasks add glamour when used for lavish curtains or throws.

bold prints

Let them stand out in a simple setting. If you are nervous of quantity, use them for just a cushion or a blind.

textile style cheapskate choice

cheap

Inexpensive cottons can be picked up in markets and the sort of shops found in the less posh areas of town. As well as pretty prints, there are stripes, spots and ginghams and many dress fabrics that tend to be cheaper anyway. Thrifty travellers will pick up Provençal prints in the South of France and colourful cottons in Asia, Africa and South America. Those who do not go abroad will find them in local ethnic shops and markets.

basic

Plain cloth is inexpensive, but its simplicity makes it nonetheless appealing. Calico is great but does shrink, so wash before sewing. Ticking has a pleasing crisp appearance, is hard-wearing and available in a variety of stripes. Denim is perfect as it is not only hard-wearing but famously improves with age. And, just as jeans go with anything from a crisp white shirt to a sexy, silky top, so denim looks comfortable in any interior.

old

No thrifty shopping excursion would be complete without a trip to the second-hand shop or a browse through the market. Thrift shops are a good source of seemingly outdated designs that only you and others in the know realise are in fact the latest thing. Bold fabrics from the 1960s and '70s, which even fairly recently wouldn't have been given house room, suddenly look perfect for cheering up a sterile space.

linen

Flat bed sheets can be bought quite cheaply and can be incorporated into curtains and covers. With new bedlinen you get a lot of fabric for your money. New flat sheets are wider than fabric bought on the roll, they come ready stitched (you could unpick the sides and thread the top edge on to a pole) and are good as generous curtains. Pure cotton is best – if you use a synthetic version it might look too much like a sheet. If you particularly like the colour and design of a duvet cover, you could always cut it up.

remnants and scraps

Dive into the remnants bins in both the furnishing and dress fabric departments for an opportunity to buy something that would otherwise be way beyond your means. It is an excuse to introduce a dash of something special by way of cushions, chair covers or for use in patchwork or appliqué.

top trimmings

Fancy trimmings are expensive, especially when it takes several metres to trim curtains or a bed cover, but there are thrifty ways of brightening up or glamorising the mundane.

make

While away a few relaxing hours making crochet flowers using up odd balls of wool bought in sales or from charity shops and market stalls.

Relive your childhood by winding wool around a circle of card to make jolly pompoms.

Knit your own trims: cast on a small number of simple stitches and just keep going.

sew

Add blanket stitch around the edges using a big needle and thick wool in a contrasting or subtly similar colour.

Bind edges with strips of printed fabric. Ideal for using up scraps, remnants and small but fabulous pieces of vintage fabrics including old clothes.

recycle

Salvage fringes, lace, buttons, ribbons and even pockets from old clothes, bedspreads, linens, cushions, shawls, scarves and lampshades.

dressing up and covering up

Good sofas and armchairs don't come cheap. It's difficult to know what to do when the condition of your sofa cover deteriorates or the shape or colour of your chair that looked perfect when you bought it suddenly doesn't live up to current expectations. New fitted covers are expensive, even if you make them yourself, but there is a way to freshen up sofas, chairs and daybeds. Think 'dressing up' rather than 'covering up' – take the fashionable layered look as your inspiration and use throws, rugs and even scarves, shawls and pashminas to mix colours and textures as you would clothes. Choose the style that suits you as well as your interior.

   The habit of throwing large bedspreads over unsavoury sofas in a desperate attempt to hide or cheer them up is common, but however carefully they are draped and tucked in they inevitably end up wrinkled and creased if you dare to sit down. Layering, using a variety of sizes and materials works better as it distracts and disguises rather than attempting a complete cover up.

smart

For a tailored look, choose smooth textures and subtle colours in cashmere, felted wool, fine weaves and plain knits. Smarten up a scruffy sofa with collar and cuffs in crisp cotton or linen for a new take on antimacassars and arm protectors.

casual

Wrap up furniture in chunky knits, crochet, fleeces, sheepskins, tartan rugs and the more subtle fake furs. Add cushions in knits, denim, cords and shaggy wools.

bo ho

You can always go hippy with Indian and African prints, plus any colourful, embroidered bits and bobs and maybe even a sheepskin.

colonial

Evoke an aura of opulence with kelims, thin Persian-style carpets and pashminas. Add an Eastern influence with jewel-coloured silk and a few tassels and fringes.

vamp

Drape fringed silk shawls over a sofa or, better still, a chaise longue. Wake up tired chairs with glamorous crushed velvet throws. Finish off with touches of silk, satin and lace.

pretty

An excuse to indulge in pretty prints, chintzes and cretonnes, as well as an opportunity to use odd lengths, remnants and scraps of fabrics to make patchwork throws, covers and cushions. Provençal prints brighten up any dull chair and spriggy flowers always look fresh. A crisp white, embroidered or lace tablecloth makes a perfect antimacassar.

sew stylish cushions and throws

There is a definite movement towards 'slow living' as a reaction against the fast, almost out-of-control pace of modern life. Many people are choosing to slow down and find time to take up creative pursuits. Indeed, crafts have undergone a renaissance and some practitioners are earning a living from painting, drawing, potting, knitting and sewing. Craftwork

sew easy

This throw was made using two inexpensive fabrics, one printed and one plain. A very cheap, fleece blanket was sandwiched in between to give a quilted look as well as extra warmth. A more quilted effect can be achieved with simple straight lines of stitching or, if inspired, a more complex decorative pattern.

pretty alternative

Antique embroidered napkins and lacy doilies are charming and can often be picked up for next to nothing. Sew two napkins together to make a pretty cover for a small pillow or cushion, then stitch a lacy doily on top of the natural crunchy linen or starched cotton.

may not be the new clubbing but it can be a fascinating and satisfying pastime. Whether you choose delicate embroidery or wild knitting, it provides the opportunity to make anything from a napkin to a bedspread using new or recycled remnants and is great for anyone interested in making something beautiful which doesn't cost a fortune.

crochet revival

Crochet is very much in vogue, so old crochet cushions and blankets are quickly snapped up in jumble sales or charity shops. Picking up some yarn and a crochet hook yourself (or asking someone else to do it for you) is the next best thing. It's easy, fun and gives you an excuse to buy some of the fabulous new wools now available.

prudent patchwork

Patchwork is popular, but the best can be pricey. Less than half a metre of fabric was enough to make these unusual cushion covers. Sew up simple pockets or sleeves in which to pop plain cushions. There's no need to to waste any fabric as individual blooms can be cut from the scraps and appliquéd onto plain fabric.

sew stylish chair flair

Fabrics have had a low profile in recent years as the plain and bare modern style replaced the drapes, pelmet and tie-back excesses of the country house look of the 1990s. Nowadays, fabric (along with knitting and crochet) is back and has brought with it a new appreciation of pattern, especially the prints from the middle decades of the last century. Patterned fabrics are creeping back onto chairs to brighten up the room, to disguise the horrors hidden beneath or to add a little more comfort. A small amount of woven or knitted fabric can go a long way to cheer up a chair, especially if used with verve and imagination.

top and tail The backs and arms of armchairs are vulnerable to wear and dirt. This modern version of the antimacassar adds a crisp, clean set of collar and cuffs to protect a new chair or cover the grubbiest parts of an old one.

fashion item The fashion for ponchos comes and goes. While they are out of favour, why not make good use of them on a chair?

office wear Office chairs don't have to wear work clothes. While they can be dressed to blend in with the surroundings, why not go for something unsuitable?

bobble hat A silly woolly hat will cheer up a plain chair and anybody's day. Get knitting.

cover-all Making tie-on covers for this type of chair is relatively easy. They can be removed for washing or a change of style.

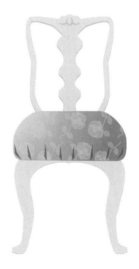

two-piece Pop a simple slip cover over the chair back, add a covered cushion to the seat and, depending on the fabric, turn an ordinary chair into a retro piece or something altogether more refined.

added comfort These fold-up chairs are a great invention, but the seat back can be uncomfortable. A small sewn pad folded over and fixed with poppers makes a world of difference.

cover-up Cut a piece of fabric big enough to cover the seat, allowing a generous border and rounding off the front corners. Hem along the edges and thread elastic through to make a semi-fitted cover.

sew stylish chair covers

Upholstery is one of the biggest furnishing costs. Good-quality sofas and armchairs are expensive but a worthwhile investment as they are generously proportioned, more comfortable and, most importantly, will last longer than cheaper alternatives. Those who choose wisely and opt for a classic shape will find it easy to fit old upholstery into new interior schemes, especially if the covers are plain and neutral.

It is possible to find a bargain old sofa or armchair that is very well made but in need of re-covering. Whether you have bought to last or bagged a bargain, a new cover will be necessary at some time either to cover worn and grubby patches or outdated patterns and colours. However, new loose covers don't come cheap and can cost as much as a new sofa, so do your sums and don't waste money if your furniture is structurally poor and the cushions and padding are saggy. Far better in that case to buy new, and if possible, buy something that will last.

made-to-measure

The fitted, tailored cover that snuggly hugs every curve and is finished with smart piping or kick pleats is a costly item. It can, however, be money well spent as the end result is a sofa or armchair that looks new and will give several more years' good service. Of course, the cost depends on the fabric and whether you make the cover yourself or have it done professionally. If you are considering doing it yourself, you really need to understand how things fit together, as well as being a proficient sewer. The cost of a professional (either an individual or a company) can be more expensive than the fabric, but will ensure a job well done.

The stretch covers often advertised extensively in the backs of magazines and colour supplements are (thankfully) no longer so popular, but many companies are now offering tailored loose covers at a reasonable rate. These are a good value-for-money option providing you have standard-shaped sofas and chairs and are prepared to choose from the fabrics available.

loose

Technically, all fitted covers are loose in that they can be removed, but a more casual, less-tailored cover is another option. Less complicated to make, loose covers are a possible DIY option (although you still need good sewing skills) as simple, unpiped seams and a plain hemmed bottom edge are easier to cope with. This variation should also be cheaper to have made as it involves less work.

baggy

The new kid on the chair-cover block is the baggy cover, which ignores the structure underneath in favour of a simplified slip cover made with fewer pieces and straighter lines. The look is in the spirit of Tuscan or Provençal farmhouses with bare floors and rustic furnishings. While they will never look smartly tailored, they can look chic if you use a plain white or neutral fabric. For anyone wishing to have a go at making their own, instructions are given on the next page.

fabric choice

Covers need to withstand a fair amount of wear and tear, especially if your household includes children, pets or couch potatoes. Good-quality, closely woven, cotton and linen will wear well, natural fibres are comfortable and if the fabric is machine-washable so much the better. A lighter-weight fabric could be used for baggy covers, but don't expect it to last long. If choosing a pattern, bear in mind the problems of lining up and matching up and allow extra fabric. Small designs will be fine but stripes and geometric patterns look better if they line up and all go in the same direction. Big checks and floral patterns also look best if they are matched, at least on the fronts of the arms.

simple chair cover

Chair covers can be complicated to make, especially if the shape of your chair is curvy rather than straight up and down. Getting something to fit all the forms takes time and skill, but fortunately a more casual cover is in vogue, which is a lot easier to make.

Ideally, upholstery fabrics should be hard-wearing, so a thicker close-weave material is usually recommended. For the novice do-it-yourself sewer, however, these fabrics are difficult to handle and the seams too much for an ordinary domestic sewing machine to cope with. Using a lighter-weight fabric will be fine as long as it isn't too flimsy. There are plenty of medium-weight cottons and linens around, both patterned and plain, but don't choose anything that obviously frays easily as the seams will be weak.

Calico is a good upholstery option as it is inexpensive but very robust, as are denim and ticking. It is always best to wash any fabric before sewing as many of them shrink – your trendy baggy cover may end up with a more fitted shape than you anticipated after its first wash.

This baggy cover is pared down to the simplest shapes, the minimum number of pieces and not too many curves. It is relatively simple to make, but take care and time. Remember – measure twice, cut once !

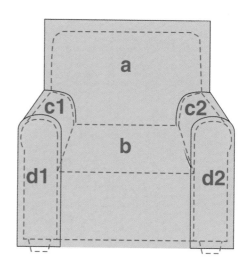

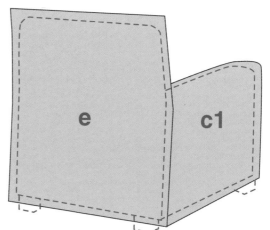

Use the diagrams above to calculate the amount of fabric needed. The best way to cut the pattern pieces is to lay the fabric, wrong side out, over the chair and mark with tailor's chalk. Cut out the pieces on a flat surface or in situ. Do not forget to leave a seam allowance of approximately 2.5 cm on all sides.

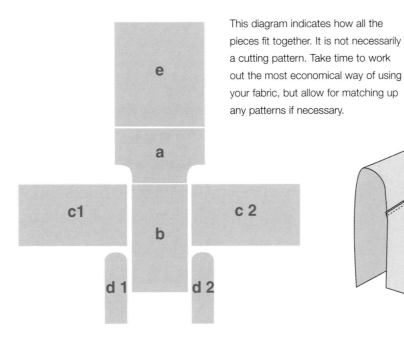

This diagram indicates how all the pieces fit together. It is not necessarily a cutting pattern. Take time to work out the most economical way of using your fabric, but allow for matching up any patterns if necessary.

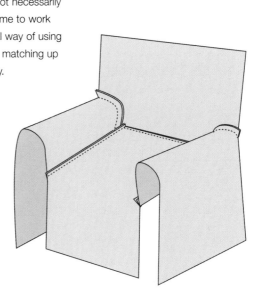

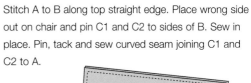

Stitch A to B along top straight edge. Place wrong side out on chair and pin C1 and C2 to sides of B. Sew in place. Pin, tack and sew curved seam joining C1 and C2 to A.

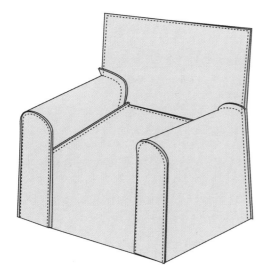

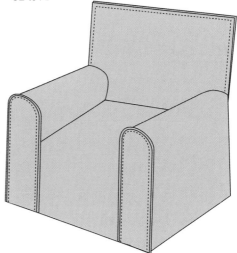

Place cover over chair. Pin and tack piece E to A across top and to C1 and C2 at sides. Pin and tack D1 and D2 to C1 and C2. Remove cover and stitch.

Turn cover right side out and place over chair. Either leave it with simple seams or add a row of stitching on the right side, around back and arms, to add definition.

budget bedheads

There is no shortage of stylish beds at bargain prices, and, although many of them look perfectly OK on their own, they can be made to look smart, special or even sexy with a small budget plus a little imagination. Choosing from a wide selection of fabrics, bedlinen, quilts, covers and cushions, you can dress up a bed in a variety of styles from crisply prim to outrageously opulent.

Your bedroom is the one private place where you can indulge in a style that is more distinctly your own. Here you have the opportunity to use fabrics in a way that may not suit the rest of your home or those who share it with you. However, you don't have to go for the frilly and flowery look. You may prefer to take your inspiration from the cool, smart, luxury-hotel style with the emphasis on plain but luxurious bedlinen and calm, restful colours.

For a crisp look, use plain linens and cottons, including denim and cord. For something completely different, use a piece of patchwork or vintage prints. For opulent luxury, go for heavy velvets or damasks or for a smart, hip-hotel look, use woollen moleskins and smooth tweeds. Keep an eye open for sales bargains and remnants in specialist shops, the dressmaking and furnishing fabric departments of bigger stores and scour antique markets and car boot sales for old curtains, linens and quilts.

Upgrade the humble divan with a luxury padded headboard. The cost of the basic materials – a piece of chipboard, wadding and tacks – is low,

though the final cost depends on the fabric used. However, it does provide an opportunity to use a fabulous, and perhaps fabulously expensive, fabric that will infuse the whole room with its sumptuousness – the amount required would be less than is needed for curtains, so by keeping the window coverings plain, you will save costs elsewhere.

A padded bedhead is relatively simple to make using a piece of chipboard covered with fabric with a layer of wadding underneath for added comfort. The size of the bedhead should be a little wider than the bed and as high as you like. Fix it at mattress height or, for a full-length version, at skirting level. When calculating the amount of wadding and fabric needed, allow for the size of the chipboard plus at least 15cm all the way around. Lightly sand any sharp, cut edges of the chipboard to prevent damage to the fabric. Cover one side of the chipboard with wadding (available from haberdashery departments) or fleece, securing it at the back with staples or small tacks. Next, cover the wadding with the chosen fabric using staples or larger-headed tacks. To

hang it securely on the wall, use hidden fixings set into the back.

A lightweight, ready-to-hang headboard can be made using an artist's canvas. Many art suppliers stock ready-made canvasses in large sizes though probably not the width of a double bed. However, they normally offer a made-to-measure service and, considering the size, the price is very reasonable. Alternatively, you can buy artists' canvas by the metre and make up your own frame using ready-cut stretchers that easily slot together. Stretching the canvas tightly and neatly requires care and a certain amount of skill, though, so only tackle it if you are good at that sort of thing. The final look is up to you and your artistic aspirations: you can leave the canvas blank, paint a picture yourself or commission one from a friendly neighbourhood artist.

5 bed ideas

For that casual, arty look, simply pin up a rectangle of fabric behind the bed. A piece of coarse linen looks suitably austere, but a scrap of velvet or damask (leave the frayed edges if you dare) adds a dash of unconventionality. For a smarter and more permanent look, sew around the edges, put eyelets along the top and hang from hooks screwed into a batten fixed to the wall.

Plain bedsteads come cheap, but sometimes they are a little too neat and shiny. Soften them by draping a quilt over the bedhead.

Layer your bed with throws, blankets and bedspreads. Don't be afraid to mix the very expensive with the dirt cheap – an old embroidered tablecloth turns a cheap plain cotton bedspread into a vintage treasure.

Sex up a plain bed with silks and satins. Why not hang curtains from a pole screwed into the ceiling? Light floaty ones are romantic but damask or velvet will add a touch of history and warmth.

Gathered valances look a bit passé; new ones are tailored to hang straight. If you don't want to sew them, simply use a throw, sheet, blanket or quilt thrown over the bed base underneath the mattress. Use as part of a layered look, mixing patterns, textures and colours.

curtains etcetera

Curtain fashions come and go, but the recent enthusiasm for a pared-down look has led to more curtains being taken down than put up. However, naked windows are an acquired taste and are neither practical nor desirable when neighbours and passers-by are close or if your room temperature plummets when there is a gentle breeze. A room can seem unfinished and cold without curtains, but they can be discreet, distinct or designer, whichever look takes your fancy.

straight up and down

Simple panels with little or no gathering, hung from plain poles or rails, are not only easy to make; they use the minimum amount of fabric. The very simplest (and perfect for shabby chic) is a piece of un-hemmed fabric hung from a bamboo cane.

opulent

Go all the way for swags and drapes in velvets, damasks and even chintz. Frighteningly expensive if new but look in sale rooms, second-hand and house clearance shops as well as curtain exchanges. Alternatively, use a very inexpensive fabric but use it generously and add tiebacks (cheap colourful cords can be found in DIY stores) and perhaps the odd tassel.

lacy and floaty

Net curtains are making a comeback. Not only do they keep out nosy neighbours; they also keep out the dust and dirt (and are much easier to wash than a slatted blind). Gathered or hung in panels, the new nets are more of a statement. Go for old or new lace, translucent cotton weaves or go glamorous with chiffon and sari fabrics.

pretty plain

Cotton or linen, printed or plain, slightly gathered on a runner or a simple pole. Works well in bedrooms where you can indulge in pretty florals. Look in street markets where you can often buy printed dress cottons very cheaply.

thermal

Keep out winter winds (and reduce the heating bills) with quilted, padded or thick lined curtains. Put a layer of wadding in between two different fabrics and quilt either with a sewing machine or by a few knotted stitches here and there.

blind

The price of ready-made blinds is impressively low. Slatted wooden or metal blinds always look smart, modern and complement most styles. Roller blinds are neat and roll out of sight during the day. On a large window, use two or three narrow ones in a row. White roller blinds are perfect for the minimal look at minimal cost. Other thrifty options are bamboo, reed and paper blinds.

These curtains are a trimmed-down version of a much-loved old pair, which were fuller and had fancy headings. The old pleated heading tape was removed and replaced with a simple tape left ungathered. New linings were made from inexpensive light-weight, fleece blankets, which keep out the cold without making the curtains heavy.

curtains something different

Bare windows may be fashionable – and the ultimate thrifty solution – but unless you are lucky enough not to be overlooked, it is not an option. The bare look can also feel cold, whereas curtains and blinds can complement the decor and complete the picture as well as screening out draughts and prying eyes.

 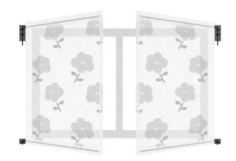 

portiere rods Window panels hung on portiere rods require a relatively small amount of fabric as there are no gathers.

Use a basic fabric and keep costs right down or indulge in a small amount of a more expensive material.

cafe continental A scrap of pretty fabric pegged to a length of curtain wire is all you need.

mix and match You may not have enough precious vintage fabric to curtain an entire window, so use it as an opportunity to display a whole collection of different designs. Don't be afraid to mix and match.

lace panel A single lace panel could be new or old, need not fit exactly and can be dyed for extra impact.

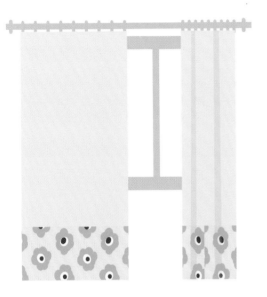

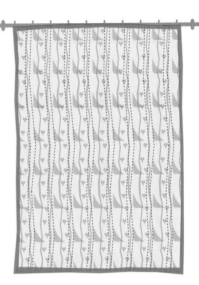

bold borders Liven up an otherwise plain pair of curtains with a border of something special or extravagant.

flimsy curtain Gather a filmy fabric skirt to a thicker fabric top, strong enough to take the curtain fittings.

quilted cosy Quilts look pretty and keep you cosy in bed and fulfil similar functions when used as a curtain.

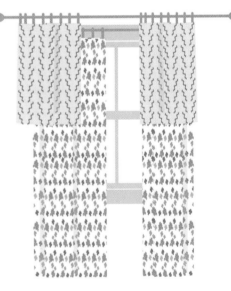

dhurries Inexpensive dhurries make great window coverings. Hang from a pole and make a feature of the fringes.

fold-back panels Hang a plain panel from simple hooks; fold it back to reveal a contrasting lining.

layer curtains Size doesn't always matter, especially if you are prepared to mix, match and use your imagination.

curtains measuring up

As there is a more relaxed attitude to curtain widths and lengths, measuring up for curtains does not have to be so crucially precise. The thrifty bonus is that the fashion for a simpler look with minimal gathering means that less fabric is required.

If you choose a patterned fabric with an obvious horizontal design, it is best to match the design on both curtains, otherwise it will look odd. Don't forget to buy extra fabric – a lot of stores will state the pattern repeat measurement, which will help you to calculate how much fabric you need. Similarly, if you are joining more than one width of fabric to make a single curtain, it will look better if you match the pattern along the seam.

If you don't want the bother of making the whole thing, go for ready-made curtains. Some are great value and can be personalised with borders, appliqué or crochet flowers, patchwork panels, fringes, buttons and bows. Inexpensive lightweight, off-the-peg curtains also make pretty, effective linings for heavier-weight curtains.

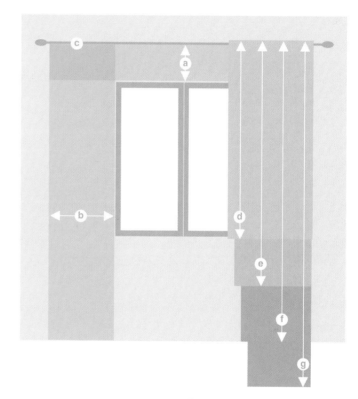

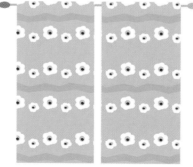

(a) height at which you hang the fitting – don't forget to allow for a gap between the pole and the curtain
(b) allow enough room for the curtains to pull back away from the window
(c) fittings
(d) sill length
(e) cropped
(f) floor length
(g) extra-long

simple curtains

If you can sew straight lines, you can make curtains. A sewing machine is useful but if you don't have one then sew by hand – it is easy and very therapeutic. Fortunately, modern curtain styles are plain rather than fussy so there is no need to tussle with the intricacies and expense of fancy headings and pleats.

To make a simple curtain, turn in approximately 1.5–2cm of fabric along both sides and then fold in again so that no raw edges are visible (using an iron makes this easier). Pin and tack in place, then stitch along the inside edge. Do the same along the top edge but fold over up to 8cm of fabric to provide space and extra strength for any header tape, curtain hooks or rings. Stitch the folded side seam.

If you want the curtain to reach to an exact position, such as the top of the window sill or the floor, turn the bottom edge last and work out the turn up with the curtains hung in place. This edge is normally hand-stitched as the fabric hangs better, but you can machine-stitch the bottom hem if preferred.

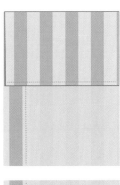

The extra weight of lined curtains makes them hang better. Make a detachable lining using touch-and-close tape.

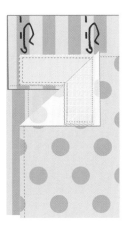

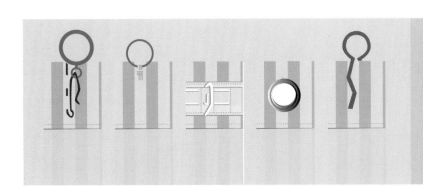

The range of hooks and rings for hanging curtains is wide. Whether your choose sew-in curtain rings, clip-on hooks or eyelets depends on the weight of your curtains and choice of rail or pole. Eyelets do not require any hooks as they thread directly onto a pole. Just make sure they fit!

thrifty fixtures and fittings

bamboo canes
Cheap as chips and available in a range of lengths from garden centres.

drawing pins
Pin fabric to the window frame for an impromptu curtain using map pins.

wooden dowelling
Thin pieces will support lightweight curtains, while the biggest will hold heavier ones with the right supports.

piping
Put up copper and plastic piping using plumbers' fittings.

bulldog clips
Good for no-fuss curtain hanging. Thread or clip on to string, cord or wire.

wire
Steel wire, strung between eyelet hooks and held taut by tensioners looks smart, minimal and modern.

plastic-coated wire
Still an easy and efficient curtain fixing.

make-do curtain ideas

If you don't want the bother of sewing, take advantage of the numerous lengths of fabric available with ready-finished edges in the form of tablecloths, sheets, throws as well as off-the peg curtains and panels. But if you are an exponent of shabby chic or the spontaneous style of interiors, don't be afraid to use fabrics in their raw unfinished states.

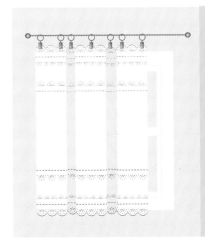

tablecloths

Tablecloths come in a wide range of fabrics, colours and designs. They come with ready-sewn edges so they can be put to use straightaway. Smaller lightweight cloths can be hung from clips or sewn-in curtain rings. Crisp, white embroidered tablecloths look pretty in bedrooms and bathrooms.

lightweight linings

If you have opted for a lightweight fabric curtain but feel the need for a little more substance, use another lightweight fabric as lining. This is useful in children's rooms as the double-thickness curtains will block out more light. You could use two sets of inexpensive, ready-made curtains tacked together.

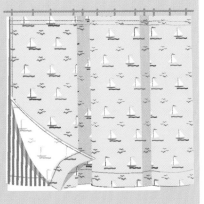

drapes

A generous length of fabric draped over a pole looks dramatic with a hint of grandeur. Anything can be used. An old linen sheet is perfect but old velvets and damasks add a dash of grand opulence.

good housekeeping fabric care

Looking after fabrics prolongs their life as well as keeping them looking good. We all frequently wash our bedlinen, but often neglect throws, covers and curtains as they aren't so easy to deal with. Dust eventually turns into dirt and it is surprising how much finds its way onto fabrics. So get into the habit of regularly vacuuming your upholstery and any heavy curtains. Natural fibres are easy to look after but anything special, such as velvets, damasks, silks and wools, should be professionally cleaned unless stated otherwise.

For cottons, linens and colour-fast dyes, the best cleaning method is machine washing with a good detergent. If you don't want to risk the super-sized machines at the launderette for large items, it may be better to get curtains and loose covers laundered professionally, especially if the fabric is expensive or the colours are likely to run.

Modern detergents cope easily with general dirt and the odd stain. Some of the biological varieties can be harsh, so stick to the non-bios and those formulated for coloureds. For very fine fabrics, such as voiles, embroideries and loose weaves, hand washing in tepid or cold water with gentle soap is advisable. Washing or cleaning instructions are usually provided when you buy new fabric, throws and cushion covers, but in the absence of such information, test a small corner first. Anything with deep colours is best washed separately at a low temperature or, for non-colour-fast dyes, in cold water.

whiter than white

Old linens are often grey or yellow but usually whiten after a few hot washes. Bedlinen and table linen will have been washed several times and therefore won't shrink – anything that doesn't survive a hot wash with a dose of detergent would not be much use anyway. Any yellow tinge can be removed by soaking in a solution of 20ml chlorine bleach to 5 litres water. Alternatively, try soaking in a bowl of warm water with two denture cleaning tablets dissolved in it. Remove mildew stains by rubbing with lemon juice and salt and leaving out in the sunshine.

ironing

You may be pleased to know that as far as bedlinen and table linen are concerned, the creased look is in. Screwed up like a rag will not do, however, it has to be an orderly crease. As soon as you take the washing out of the machine, shake all items and pull into shape. When dry, fold neatly and smooth down by hand. Except for large or expensive items, sending ironing to a laundry or getting someone else to do it are not very thrifty options. For unwieldy amounts of fabric or awkward shapes such as loose covers, you can iron them in situ using a steamer, formerly used by professionals but now available for domestic use.

upholstery

There are a number of proprietary products for DIY upholstery cleaning, but don't attempt it unless you know what you are doing – the foam, wadding or feathers underneath may react badly to the wrong cleaning method. Look for a care label and use appropriate products accordingly. If in doubt, get it done professionally.

professional cleaning

For luxury fabrics, professional cleaning is the best option. Dry cleaning is the usual method and, though expensive, the items do get pressed as well – something that can be tricky to do yourself.

Steam cleaning by a professional company is recommended for upholstery with fixed covers. The cleaner normally does the job in your home.

repairing

While threadbare patches can add charm, they reduce the life of sofas and chairs, so get out your sewing kit to darn and patch. A spare piece of matching fabric is perfect for patching or for the dilapidated look a contrasting pattern or plain will do nicely.

save energy

Being thrifty is not only about spending less; it also involves questioning and reassessing your priorities and addressing the wider implications of how you choose to spend your money. For some, cutting down on consumption is a necessity, while for others it offers an opportunity to adopt a different attitude to life, whether approached from a personal or global perspective.

the 're-' issue

The mantra of energy conservation and eco-consideration is reduce, reuse and recycle. There are many more 're-' issues that benefit not only our environment but also our personal wellbeing.

It's not a bad idea to stop and re-evaluate your life from time to time. Personal circumstances change, as do ambitions and aspirations, and in today's competitive market there is no certainty of economic stability. Many people are choosing to downshift – sometimes of necessity in order to cope with changes in work situations, relationships, marriage, children or retirement – whilst others are making a conscious decision to improve their quality of life by reducing the stress caused by trying to keep up with financial commitments.

The dictionary definition of thrift refers to frugality and economical management, which may sound rather worthy. However, it can be a liberating experience to care less for material possessions and more for your health, wealth and happiness. Adopting a holistic approach to 're-' issues involves taking into account the state of your mind as well as that of your bank balance. Reconsider where you live, how you live and what you live for. Think positively and imaginatively – readjusting your aspirations to bring them into line

with your income doesn't have to mean exchanging designer labels and meals out for sackcloth and gruel. Taking a look at your finances, how you use them and where you could save is a worthwhile exercise, and even if you are not prepared to make any sacrifices the exercise may spur you on to earning more money!

A thrifty approach is not just about cutting down and doesn't always have to mean change. Thrift is more about reconsidering your priorities, changing direction and, perhaps, thinking laterally. If you are a fashion freak, for example, it isn't necessary to forgo the latest trends. Following fashion can be enormous fun, but it also contributes to a vibrant, forward-looking, forward-thinking society. Design is no longer regarded simply as a ornament, but is acknowledged as an industry that uses innovation and invention to create better, and often cheaper, products.

Thrift is currently very fashionable and there is no longer any stigma attached to buying second-hand – though it has put the prices up, which makes it even more important to stay ahead of the game. So being fashionable can be good for you, your pocket and the world. Pursuing a thrifty lifestyle is very 'à la mode'.

10 Rs

reduce

Think before you spend your money, reduce your intake and use less resources. Pause for thought before you buy and consider whether you will benefit from the purchase. Buy what you need rather than what you want.

revive

Reawaken old passions by reviving past interests in hobbies, sports, artistic activities and other pastimes. Anything from knitting to kite flying, jogging to jiving can bring you pleasure and the cost needn't be high.

reorganise

Save time, money and your temper by reorganising your home, your possessions and your habits. Make sure there is somewhere to put everything, and anything that is used frequently is kept to hand.

reuse

Buy a reusable 'bag for life' from the supermarket, then use any additional plastic bags as bin liners. Instead of disposables, buy washable cotton nappies, handkerchiefs and dishcloths that consume less raw materials.

reinvent

As well as putting old furniture to new uses and turning old clothes and fabrics into cushion covers and patchwork quilts, think big and reinvent the way you use your home to make it more practical, pleasing and energy efficient.

reclaim

Old floorboards, bricks and window frames can be reused, so either recycle or sell them on. Reclaimed materials, which are often better quality and nicer looking than new equivalents, are sometimes cheaper.

recycle

Glass, newspaper, plastic, cans and other items can be given a new lease of life. Recycling centres and local authorities redistribute computers, electrical appliances, furniture, clothes and books to good causes.

refresh and reinvigorate

Tired homes need little more than a good clean and a coat of paint to reawaken your interest. Rather than splashing out on something new, reinvigorate a room by moving the furniture around.

relax

Have a night in with a good book, television programme or cosy chat. Eating out is fun but expensive. For the cost of a main course, feast on bread, cheeses, meats and patisserie, which don't require any cooking.

rethink

Re-evaluate the way you live your life, from your diet and dress to your home life and work life. Instead of shopping during lunch, visit museums or galleries where you can often view the permanent collections for free.

conserve, create and support

We are constantly exhorted to 'Save the Planet'. In truth, the planet will survive whatever we throw at it, which is more than can be said for the human race. Conservation has become a global issue. Whatever your views or understanding, it is widely agreed that reducing energy consumption makes good thrift sense.

power and fuel

Turn off appliances at the plug – the standby state uses a surprising amount of electricity. Don't waste energy boiling more water than you need – fill the kettle only with what you require. A-rated washing appliances are inherently energy efficient, but use them efficiently too by ensuring there is always a full load, using a low-temperature wash cycle and, if available, an economy wash. Transport is the biggest user of energy, so keep car journeys to the essential and, where possible, walk, cycle or get the bus.

heat

Look at the big picture and make sure your home is well insulated. Loft insulation is easy to put in place, wall insulation is not so straightforward, but if you are buying or renovating a home it is worth considering. Flax, cellulose and materials made from recycled paper and wool are eco-options. Fit thermostats on all radiators, turn radiators off in rooms you are not using and keep the doors shut. In cold months, think about moving into a different, smaller room that is easier and cheaper to heat. You may like bare windows but an enormous amount of heat is lost through glass and badly fitting frames. Thick and generous curtains that cover the whole window frame will not only keep in the heat but also make a room feel warmer. A curtain over a door will also keep out the cold. Velvet or heavy cotton is good but try a blanket or throw, or a fleece, which is very light and easy to hang in place. Fit draught excluders on outside doors – choose one to suit your door and door frame. Zap that gale under the door with a knitted sausage dog.

light

Save energy and switch off unnecessary lights and don't leave lights on in empty rooms. However, a low level of light can be depressing and not good for the eyes (and for safety make sure that steps or stairs are well lit), so use a good task light for reading, working and cooking and fit energy-saving bulbs where possible.

water

Flushing comprises 35 per cent of household water consumption; installing a water-efficient loo uses only half as much water per flush. Alternatively, fill a bottle with water and place it in your cistern. A shower uses less water than a bath and turn the tap off while you actually brush your teeth. If you have a garden, catch the rainwater for watering plants by rerouting the downpipe to a large plastic or metal tank, dustbin or purpose-bought rainwater butt. You could install a 'rain harvester' on the downpipe, which filters the water and diverts it to a butt or storage tank for use for the washing machine and flushing loos as well as the garden.

health

Thrift doesn't always mean choosing the cheapest and, where health is concerned, this is not a time for penny-pinching. And with worries about allergies, harmful chemical pollutants and VOCs (volatile organic compounds), it makes sense to pay a little more for the healthy option. Go for 'natural' paints with ingredients made from renewable natural minerals and earth and mineral pigments as they allow the wall to breathe, avoiding condensation problems and therefore better for both your home and your body. Healthy versions of plaster, flooring materials and fibreboards are also available and demand and legislation are helping to bring the prices down. Walking, running and cycling are healthy activities and much cheaper than joining a gym.

solar power

There is satisfaction and money to be gained if you produce even a tiny amount of the power you consume. The statistics regarding the cost efficiency of solar panels are confusing, but any reduction in bills is welcome and it is silly to let all that sunlight go to waste. Installation is costly and therefore a long-term investment, although as we are living in a time of energy crises, solar panels may well increase the resale value of your house. On a smaller scale it is now possible to buy a number of solar-powered gadgets and gizmos including garden lights.

wind power

Wind farms are popping up all over, but you don't need to live on a hill to benefit from this renewable energy source. As well as buying your energy from wind-power suppliers (use the internet for details), you can also get small domestic-size windmills. They vary in size, price and capacity to run anything from most of your domestic requirements to small amounts for outdoor lighting. Installing a windmill may need planning permission (as well as consent from the neighbours), so do your research. Local authorities and manufacturers will help.

food

Grow your own vegetables. If you are not lucky enough to have a garden, you can still grow tomatoes on a balcony, herbs on a window sill, potatoes in a dustbin, courgettes and runner beans in large pots. If you do have a garden, recycle waste to make compost.

fair trade

Don't just recycle your rubbish; buy products made from recycled materials, including glass, paper and plastic. Buy timber from renewable resources – look for the FSC mark of the World Wildlife Fund's Forest Stewardship Council. Buy Fair Trade items to ensure producers get the best price for their hard work.

stay local

Cut transport costs (your own plus those of retail industries) by buying local produce where possible. Support local shops and markets. Join community schemes and activities such as car shares.

money

All the foregoing can save you money. Simply not spending saves even more, but in today's retail environment spending can be addictive. Noone is suggesting going without, but remind yourself to buy what you 'need' rather than 'want'. Being thrifty can give personal satisfaction and reduce anxiety as well as overdrafts.

easy energy savers

energy-efficient bulbs

They use 75 per cent less energy and last up to 12 times longer than normal bulbs. They are more expensive, so buy in bulk via mail order to save money. The range of sizes available is now very wide, so there's no excuse not to use them.

a-rated electrical appliances

Choose A-rated items, including fridges, freezers, washing machines and dishwashers. They are more efficient in the amount of power they use and, in the case of washing, the amount of water.

condensing boiler

The initial installation cost is higher than a standard boiler, but they cut energy consumption by up to 4 per cent.

wind-up radio

The clockwork radio was originally invented for use in remote areas of the world where no power was available, but the fact that they don't need batteries gives them added eco-cred. Look out for wind-up mobile phone chargers too.

solar-powered garden lighting

Solar panels may be out of the question for your home, but consider installing small versions to run your garden lights. Don't expect a high level of illumination, but who wants that in a garden anyway.

cheap organisers

bulldog clips

Organise anything from bills to photos
using a selection of bulldog clips in
different sizes and colours. Either hang
them on hooks or string behind a door
or display them as a feature.

plastic folders

Keep papers safe and orderly by
filing them in clearly labelled plastic
folders which can be kept neatly in a
filing cabinet, drawer or large box.
If you can't cope with frequent filing,
put everything in a pending folder
so things don't go astray.

ring binders

Instead of keeping an unruly pile of
papers, punch holes in everything
and put them in ring binders where
they can be quickly filed, can't fall
out and get lost. File papers by subject
in different coloured binders on a shelf
that can be easily accessed.

bags and baskets

If you can't resist buying another bag
or basket, use them as storage. Hang
them on a row of hooks where you
can access the contents easily, or line
them up on a shelf to make a display.

magazine files

Ideal for filing away papers as they are
easy to pop things into. Buy one for
each category – bills, pending, filing – or
for each household or family member.

get organised

If you are organised, you will save both time and money, and life will be less fraught if everything from important papers to PE kit can be found in the right place at the right time. You don't have to be an organisation freak but a little discipline and a few storage products will result in a well-organised house that is more relaxed and efficient – and probably looks nicer too.

A jumble of carelessly stored possessions are at risk of being lost or damaged as well as mislaid, and items such as clothes, utensils, tools and treasures will last longer if they are properly stored and cared for. Something as simple as a hook near the door for your keys or a large ceramic bowl for bunging bills in can save time, and tempers, when next you need to leave the house or pay your dues.

Organise your kitchen so that frequently used utensils and gadgets are to hand and food is stored in visible and appetising order. Keep tools together either in a purpose-made toolbox or hanging on hooks or a rack where you can find them and they won't get damaged.

Rethink your rubbish disposal and recycle as much as possible. Make it easier for yourself and any others in the household with a system of receptacles for each recyclable material. A set of different-coloured bins will look cheerful in a kitchen, or outside in a yard or garden, but if space is limited use large baskets which will look good in a hallway or living room. State your eco-virtues with a row of brightly coloured, labelled bags available from mail-order companies (or make your own) and save valuable floor space by hanging them from sturdy hooks screwed to the wall.

If you have a garden, a compost heap is a must and there are plenty of containers and systems, for both indoors and out, to ensure the production of good compost, rather than a soggy, smelly heap.

Clothes will last longer if they are looked after by hanging them up and putting them away (which can also save on washing as clothes left lying around are often put in the washing machine when they are not really dirty) and you will save time finding and choosing what to wear if you organise them into groups by colour or type of use.

paperwork

Being able to find important papers or documents can also save you from potential delays, trouble and possible fines. Make sure all legal documents are filed away in an accessible and safe place. It's a good idea to keep passports, certificates etc. in a metal, fireproof box.

Don't hide bills away in the hope that they will pay themselves; keep them on a bulldog clip in an obvious place to remind you to deal with them. If possible always pay on time to avoid penalties or extra interest. Direct debit is a convenient way of paying bills and many companies and organisations offer discount incentives if you pay by this method, so take advantage wherever possible.

reaping the benefits

What you get out of being thrifty will depend on how widely you apply the philosophy. There is bound to be some benefit or saving, be it small enough to allow an extra treat or big enough to change your whole life.

new look

If you follow the advice in this book, you may achieve a newly stylish home that not only looks better but feels and works better too. The same principles applied to your clothes could turn you into a more together fashionista.

new interests

Giving up expensive nights out is one way of saving money, but you don't have to stay in. For the cost of one night's clubbing, you could enrol at a local evening class to study just about anything, from IT to tango, keep-fit to yoga. Alternatively, go jogging, which is free, and spend the money saved on pursuing those latent talents in pottery, painting or textiles classes. Now is the time to take up dancing. Discos are dull compared to jive, tango or tap. Why not indulge in the newly popular ballroom dancing (and go to dressmaking classes to make your own sequinned number)? As it is never too late to learn, use some

of your hard-saved cash to buy that musical instrument you have hankered after – and get playing.

Local societies can be fun. The price of one theatre ticket could well be more than a whole year's subscription to the local amateur dramatic society where you can indulge your thespian ambitions on the stage or behind the scenes. The whole experience could result in much more drama than you would get in an evening in the West End.

If you enjoy enjoy gardening, rip up the decking and gravel and replace it with a vegetable patch. It can supply you with produce throughout the year, while providing a pleasurable way to fill evenings and weekends.

new life

The smallest change in lifestyle can lead to a big, life-changing decision. Many people are downshifting from stressful, high-paid jobs to part-time or lower-paid employment, which offers more free time and satisfaction in place of money. Some are also moving from expensive properties to a either smaller spaces in the town, which offer more in the way of local facilities and cuts down on travel, or to bigger spaces with, perhaps, a garden in a cheaper area. Others are

opting out and taking on the challenge of a new, alternative life in the countryside or abroad.

Nowadays, few people expect to remain in one job or career, and retraining can bring about a different direction or better prospects. Pursuing a thrifty lifestyle can free up money to pay for this training and could result in a larger or more regular income, or just a nicer life.

New interests can lead to new business opportunities. You may find that your prowess at pottery propels you into a career as an artist or shop-owner or an IT course provides you with enough expertise to start a small home business.

new attitude

Eschewing consumerism in favour of lower outgoings should bring peace of mind and freedom from some of the pressures of modern-day life. It can also raise awareness of the wider world, including issues of the environment, the economy, the need to conserve resources and the need for sustainability. In addition you may become more aware of the needs and problems of others, all of which might change your attitude to the world in general and make you feel you want to do your bit either as a voluntary worker, an eco-campaigner, or working for a charity. This could involve work abroad, spending a weekend reclaiming a meadow or spending a few hours a week working for the local care home or Citizens Advice Bureau.

something special

Spending money isn't a sin; in fact it keeps the economy going, so why not spend money saved on the mundane on something beautiful such as a work of art, or something special such as a fantastic holiday of a lifetime? However, some of the best things in life are free, and a little extra cash or extra time will enable you to appreciate more fully the landscape, a blue sky or the opportunity to relax and enjoy a better life.

thrift directory

diy superstores

B&Q
tel 0845 309 3099
www.diy.com

FOCUS DO IT ALL
tel 0800 436 436
www.focusdoitall.co.uk

HOMEBASE
tel 0845 300 1768
www.homebase.co.uk

WICKES
tel 0870 608 9001
www.wickes.co.uk

planning

BUILDING CENTRE
26 Store Street
London WC1E 7BT
tel 09065 161136 (calls
charged at £1.50 per minute)
www.buildingcentre.co.uk

ROYAL INSTITUTE OF BRITISH
ARCHITECTS (RIBA)
Client Services
66 Portland Place
London W1B 1AD
tel 020 7307 3700
fax 020 7436 9112
www.architecture.com

architectural salvage and reclamation

LASSCO
Clergy House, Mark Street
London EC2A 4ER
tel 020 7749 9944
www.lassco.co.uk

RETROUVIUS
2a Ravensworth Road
London NW10 5NR
tel 020 8960 6060
www.retrouvius.com

SALVO!
www.salvoweb.com
*'wanted' as well as
'for sale' listings*

WALCOT RECLAMATION AND
ARCHITECTURAL ANTIQUES
108 Walcot Street
Bath, Avon BA1 5BG
tel 01225 444404
www.walcot.com

heating

CENTRE FOR ALTERNATIVE
TECHNOLOGY
Machynlleth
Powys SY20 9AZ
tel 01654 705989
www.cat.org.uk

COUNCIL OF REGISTERED
GAS INSTALLERS (CORGI)
tel 08705 168111
www.shop.corgi_gas.com

ECOLOGY BUILDING SOCIETY
tel 0845 674 5566
www.ecology.co.uk
*mutual building society
promoting sustainable housing
and sustainable communities*

ENERGY EFFICIENCY ADVICE
CENTRE
136 Upper Street
London N1 1QP
tel 0845 727 7200
for helpline
www.saveenergy.co.uk
*advice on how to save energy
and money in the home*

THE GREEN BUILDING STORE
11 Huddersfield Road
Meltham, Holmfirth
West Yorkshire HD9 4NJ
tel 01484 854 898
www.greenbuildingstore.co.uk
*environmentally friendly loft
insulation made from recycled
newspaper; a non-toxic, solvent-
free paint and varnish stripper*

flooring

ALTERNATIVE FLOORING CO.
tel 01264 335111
www.alternativeflooring.com

FOREST STEWARDSHIP
COUNCIL (FSC)
www.fsc-uk.info
*the FSC logo confirms that
wood is from a sustainably
managed forest, rather than
part of the vast trade in illegally
logged old-growth forest*

NATURAL WOOD FLOOR CO.
20 Smugglers Way
London SW18
tel 020 8871 9771

SOLID FLOOR LTD
128 St John Street
London EC1V 4JS
tel 020 7251 2917
www.solidfloor.co.uk

eco-friendly paints

AURO ORGANIC PAINTS
tel 01452 772020
www.auroorganic.co.uk

COMMUNITY RE>PAINT
www.communityrepaint.org.uk
*diverts unwanted paint to local
groups and charities. An*

*estimated 75 million litres of
paint are put into landfill sites
each year, depleting ground
water and ozone*

FARROW AND BALL
Uddens Estate
Wimborne, Dorset BH21 7NL
tel 01202 876141
for stockists nationwide
fax 01202 873793
www.farrow-ball.com

GEORGINA BARROW
NATURAL PAINTS
www.gbnaturalpaints.co.uk

NUTSHELL NATURAL PAINTS
PO Box 72
South Brent TQ10 9YR
tel 01364 73801

bathrooms

IDEAL STANDARD
tel 01482 346461
www.ideal-standard.co.uk
*special range of bathroom
fittings for small spaces*

kitchens

CRABTREE KITCHENS
The Sorting Office
17 Station Road
London SW13 0LF
tel 020 8392 6955
www.crabtreekitchens.co.uk
Also at:
Twickenham 020 8755 1121
Bristol 01179 292293
Dumfriesshire 01387 740288

HABITAT
tel 08456 010740 for
branches nationwide
www.habitat.net

IKEA UK LTD
tel 020 8208 5600
for branches nationwide
www.ikea.com

contemporary and classic furniture

ARAM
110 Drury Lane
London WC2
tel 020 7557 7557
www.aram.co.uk

THE CONRAN SHOP
tel 020 7589 7401
for branches
www.conran.com
modern furniture, lighting, fabrics and accessories

HOMESPUN
www.homespunvintagedesign.co.uk
the best of post-war British design at affordable prices

ISOKON PLUS
Turnham Green Terrace Mews
London W4 1QU
tel 020 8994 0636
www.isokonplus.com
classic and contemporary bent wood furniture

SCP
135–139 Curtain Road
London EC2A 3BX
tel 020 7739 1869
fax 020 7729 4224
www.scp.co.uk

VITSOE
72 Wigmore Street
London W1
tel 020 7935 4968
www.vitsoe.com
Dieter Rams' classic 606 Universal Shelving System

antique and flea markets

BATH FLEA MARKET
Tram Shed, Walcot Street,
Bath, Avon
saturdays

BERMONDSEY ANTIQUE MARKET
corner of Long Lane and
Bermondsey Street,
London SE1
fridays from 5a.m.

BRIGHTON MARKET
car park behind railway station
sundays 5a.m. to noon

fabrics and soft furnishings

CURTAIN DESIGN AND AGENCY
www.thecurtainagency.co.uk
made-to-measure curtains as well as second-hand curtains

CURTAIN EXCHANGE
www.thecurtainexchange.net
for branches nationwide
bespoke and ready-made curtains and blinds as well as second-hand curtain service

RUSSELL AND CHAPPLE LTD
23 Monmouth Street
London WC1 9DD
tel 020 7836 7521
www.randc.net
natural linens, cottons, calico and deckchair canvas

Z. BUTT TEXTILES LTD
24 Brick Lane
London E1 6RL
tel 020 7247 7776
cheap plain calicos, muslins and tickings

storage

THE HOLDING COMPANY
243–245 Kings Road
London SW3 5EL
tel 020 7352 1600
storage specialists

MUJI
tel 020 7494 1197
for stockists and mail order
modern Japanese storage and stationery

second-hand goods

EBAY
www.ebay.com
on-line auction site

CAR BOOT CALENDAR
www.carbootcalendar.com
a national directory of car boot sales

LOOT
www.loot.com
on-line edition of listings magazine

charity shops

ASSOCIATION OF CHARITY SHOPS
www.charityshops.org.uk
a national directory of charity shops

FURNITURE RECYCLING NETWORK
c/o Community Furniture Service
The Old Drill Hall
17a Vicarage Street North
Wakefield WF1 4JS
tel 0116 233 7007
for information about recycling projects

OXFAM
www.oxfam.org.uk
for branches nationwide

transport

SMART MOVES
www.smartmoves.co.uk
pay-as-you-drive car club. Each club car typically replaces five privately owned vehicles

gardening

NATIONAL SOCIETY OF ALLOTMENT AND LEISURE GARDENERS
www.nsalg.org.uk
with your own allotment your vegetables won't be jet-lagged by the time they hit your plate

COMMUNITY COMPOSTING NETWORK
www.communitycompost.org
provides a wealth of information and details of local schemes for those without gardens. Up to 60 per cent of average household rubbish can be composted

fashion

TRAID (TEXTILE RECYCLING FOR AID)
www.traid.org.uk
outlets in London and brighton

index

author's acknowledgements

Many thanks to my excellent fellow team members: Mary the wonderfully fastidious art director and Lisa the perfect editor, who are both enthusiastic and fully paid-up members of the thrift club. Thanks also to Jane O'Shea for going with the idea.

publisher's acknowledgements

The publisher has made every effort to trace the copyright holders, architects and designers featured in this book. We apologise in advance for any unintentional omission and would be pleased to insert the appropriate acknowledgement in any subsequent edition.

2–10 Graham Atkins Hughes; 13 James Mortimer/*The World of Interiors*; 14 Graham Atkins Hughes; 16 Hotze Eisma; 18–21 Graham Atkins Hughes; 25 Uli Schade/*Elle Decoration*; 27 Hotze Eisma/Taverne Agence/*Elle Decoration*; 28–32 Graham Atkins Hughes; 37 Hotze Eisma; 38–54 Graham Atkins Hughes; 58 Ray Main/Mainstream; 64–72 Graham Atkins Hughes; 78 Antony Crolla/*The World of Interiors*; 81 James Mortimer/*The World of Interiors*; 83–91 Graham Atkins Hughes; 92 Hotze Eisma; 96 Graham Atkins Hughes; 99 David Hiscock/Robert Montgomery & Partners; 100 Luke White/Interior Archive; 102–111 Graham Atkins Hughes; 114 Hotze Eisma; 119–121 Graham Atkins Hughes; 126 Bernard Touillon/*The World of Interiors*; 129–136 Graham Atkins Hughes.